TWAYNE'S WORLD AUTHORS SERIES
A Survey of the World's Literature

FRANCE

Maxwell A. Smith, Guerry Professor of French, Emeritus
The University of Chattanooga
Former Visiting Professor in Modern Languages
The Florida State University

EDITOR

Honoré De Balzac

TWAS 541

Honoré De Balzac

HONORÉ DE BALZAC

By DIANA FESTA–McCORMICK

*Brooklyn College of the City
University of New York*

TWAYNE PUBLISHERS
A DIVISION OF G. K. HALL & CO., BOSTON

Published in 1979 by Twayne Publishers,
A Division of G. K. Hall & Co.

Printed on permanent/durable acid-free paper and bound
in the United States of America

First Printing

Library of Congress Cataloging in Publication Data

Festa-McCormick, Diana.
Honoré de Balzac.

(Twayne's world authors series ; TWAS 541 : France)
Bibliography: p. 175-181.
Includes index.
1. Balzac, Honoré de, 1799-1850
— Criticism and interpretation.
PQ2181.F44   843'.7   78-31882
ISBN 0-8057-6383-X

Contents

About the Author

The author of this volume has already published, in French, a volume on Balzac's short stories (Nizet, 1973), which was honored by the French Academy (Prix Guizot). She has a volume on *The City as a Catalyst* due to appear in Spring 1979 (Associated University Presses of New Jersey). She has written in American, French, and Italian journals close to twenty articles, on Hugo, Balzac, Verlaine, Flaubert, Gide, Proust, Char and other writers. She received her PhD degree at the Graduate Center of the City University of New York in 1973 and has taught for several years Comparative and French literature at Brooklyn College. She has traveled abroad widely and given many papers at scholars' conferences and colloquia in the United States.

Preface

The attempt to do a comprehensive study of Balzac in the limited space allowed by the Twayne series is perplexing. No writer in the whole of French literature, with the possible exception of Zola and Hugo, has produced so large a number of outstanding works, so varied in their aim and content. Between the years 1830 and 1842, Balzac wrote some eighty works that included, among others, *La Peau de Chagrin, Louis Lambert, Eugénie Grandet, La Recherche de l'Absolu, Le Père Goriot, Le Lys dans la Vallée, Les Illusions perdues, Béatrix,* and several short stories among the most striking ever written. The opinion of critics is uncertain in the selection of what might be considered "the" masterpieces in his production. No *Madame Bovary* or *Le Rouge et le Noir* clearly comes to mind, as in the case of Flaubert and Stendhal. Perhaps the only way to appraise Balzac is, as he himself wished, through his *Comédie Humaine* as a whole, the complex volumes in which he meandered through the many labyrinths of the soul and man's social condition. Balzac is the creator of a world that was both peculiarly his own and that embraced magically the expanse of unrecorded history. Life's contradictions, the disparity between man's wishes and his nature, all that he wanted to capture and hold fast for generations to come. The intensity of his vision made him labor feverishly, in a sustained and passionate contemplation of his imaginary universe. Through the sheer bulk and variety of his work, the vast number of plots and characters that he created, and his impact on men as diverse as Dostoevsky, Marx, Engels, Zola, Proust, Heinrich Mann, Henry James, Faulkner, and Dreiser, he stands at the very center of modern fiction. As the twentieth century draws to its close and ever since a wealth of critical and scholarly publications hailed and followed the centenary of his death in 1950, the novelist looms more assured than ever of perennial fame.

The difficulties of encompassing in one small volume the dramatic career of Balzac and his eighty or hundred works are immense. To follow the classification proposed by the author, but repeatedly modified or disregarded by him, would be artificial; so would an austere neglect of the biography and of the psychology of Balzac in favor of an exclusive concentration on the novels, their fictional technique and language. When all is said, the vitality of Balzac's temperament, his almost superhuman power of living his plots, his dreams, his loves, his sorrows, blending the man with the author, lie at the very spring of his genius. It may be easy to find fault with Balzac as a philosopher, just as it is with the ideas of any other novelist, if the critic severs them from the intensity of the passion with which those ideas were lived. Still, there was in the novelist a thinker who was true to his imperious aphorism that "it is not enough to be a man; one must be a system." A number of admirers of Balzac have stressed in him the imaginative creator and the visionary, two terms dear to our contemporaries who are fond of probing into the arcana of "l'imaginaire." But the portrayer of a whole society, the social critic, even the realist and the historical novelist, are no less notable.

It was unavoidable, in the chapters which follow, to pay only scant attention to some aspects of the Balzacian achievements: the dramatic works, the correspondence — second only to Flaubert's in bulk and in interest among novelists' letters — the rich and relatively neglected critical essays of Balzac, and the early novels, signed with pseudonyms, often meretricious and hasty exercises written for money, yet occasionally revealing of the author's gifts. The very great Balzac is that of some fifteen or twenty novels, none of them faultless, all of them striking, original, profound, and of short stories which count among the finest in the language. The main body of this volume concentrates on what in Balzac is powerful, unique, and likely to go down to the ages. Our problem, predictably, was one of selection — and hence of painful elimination. Too many notable works had to be put aside, keeping in mind that other stories offered perhaps similar points in a more representative manner. *Le Cousin Pons,* for instance, was given up for *La Cousine Bette*; the robust humor of *Gaudissart* or *César Birotteau* was renounced in favor of *La Vieille Fille.* Such remarkable works as *Honorine, Béatrix, La Rabouilleuse* were reluctantly neglected; the whole "mystical" and Swedenborgian Balzac — such as is found in *Séraphita* — was sacrificed and only alluded to in our brief study of *Louis Lambert* and *La Recherche de l'Absolu.*

The subject of Balzac as a master of the short story technique

Preface

should have deserved a separate chapter; this too was finally left out, with the consideration that I had already published a volume on that subject. The role of the artist in Balzac's stories, from "Gambara" to "Le Chef d'Oeuvre inconnu" and *La Rabouilleuse,* so convincingly and thoroughly presented by Pierre Laubriet, found no room in our study. We have concentrated on only a few of the best known works in Balzac's enormous opus, on a general presentation of the author in his own times and his growing reputation in ours. Our main intention has been to attract readers, and to reinforce the appreciation of old admirers, for one of the most inventive and accomplished novelists of all times.

For the sake of clarity, we have left all titles in their original French; English translations have often proved somewhat enigmatic and confusing. The Penguin edition of *La Rabouilleuse,* for instance, gives it the title *Black Sheep. La Peau de Chagrin* is indifferently called *The Wild Ass's Skin* or *The Magic Skin* in various translations. Other titles are not readily recognizable: *The Commission of Lunacy* for *L'Interdiction, Pinpricks of Married Life* for *Petites Misères de la Vie conjugale.* Generous use has been made of the many works of scholarship on Balzac, and the most valuable of them are mentioned in our bibliography. But our aim has been to remain clear and suggestive, and to avoid pedantry. We hope to assist the readers in their understanding of Balzac, in admiring the best in him while eschewing ponderousness.

Our thanks go to Professor Maxwell A. Smith, who kindly gave wise counsel and encouragement. This book in the Twayne series of French authors was originally to have been written by Professor J. A. Bédé who was long prevented from doing it by other assignments, and eventually by his death in January 1977. The author expresses her gratitude to that great teacher with whom she exchanged views on *La Comédie Humaine.*

With deep affection and admiration, this short study is dedicated to a dearest friend and master, Henri Peyre.

DIANA FESTA-MCCORMICK

Chronology

1799   Honoré de Balzac born in Tours, May 20.

1800   Birth of his sister Laure (later, de Surville), September 29.

1807   Birth of his brother Henri, probably adulterous son of Jean de Margonne, owner of the Château of Saché, December 21.

1807– Balzac is a boarder at the School of the Oratorians at
1813   Vendôme. Hardly ever visited by his family, goes through a brief crisis of mysticism.

1814   The Balzac family moves to Paris.

1816– Honoré works as law clerk with Guyonnet de Merville, who
1819   becomes Derville in the novels. In 1819 a brother of his father is guillotined at Albi, as a murderer.

1819   Honoré lives alone in a shabby attic in Rue Lesdiguières, near the Bastille. Begins writing.

1820   Moves with his family to Villeparisis, east of Paris, near Meaux, writes a tragedy in verse, *Cromwell,* and meets Mme de Berny, twenty-two years older than he, who lavishes love, devotion, and assistance on him.

1821– Writes several novels under different pseudonyms.
1824

1825– Launches into a business career as editor of French classics,
1827   then as printer and publisher; runs into heavy debts. Becomes friends with a devoted admirer of his, Zulma Carraud, whom he will often visit in Angoulême, then in Issoudum. Has a liaison with the Duchess of Abrantès, widow of General Junot, who had been close to Napoleon.

1829   Honoré's father dies. After a stay at Fougères, in Britanny, writes his first important novel on the civil war in Vendée, *Les Chouans.* His *Physiologie du Mariage,* in a risqué, satirical vein, arouses lively discussion.

1830   Writes prolifically in newspapers, goes into society, travels with Mme de Berny, the "Dilecta."

1831– Scores his first resounding success with *La Peau de Chagrin.*
1832   Intensive work and publication of many short stories of the first *Contes drolatiques,* written in sixteenth-century

manner. Publishes a philosophical and autobiographical novel, *Louis Lambert.* Attempt at a love affair with the Marquise de Castries.

1833   Publication of *Le Médecin de Campagne.* Receives several letters signed "L'Etrangère" from the Polish Countess Hanska. Meets her in Neuchatel, in September, then in Geneva in December. Publication of *Eugénie Grandet, Ferragus.*

1834   Fiercely intensive work, busy social life; meets Sarah Lovell, an English lady whose married name is Countess Guidoboni-Visconti. She becomes his mistress and has a child, probably by him. Two of his most renowned novels appear, *La Recherche de l'Absolu* and *Père Goriot.*

1835   Hunted by creditors, lives in hiding. *La Fille aux Yeux d'Or, Le Lys dans la Vallée.* Meets Countess Hanska and her husband in Vienna in May.

1836   Founds a periodical, *Chronique de Paris,* which soon fails. Travels in Italy. Learns the news of the death of "La Dilecta."

1837   Buys a house, "Les Jardies," near Sèvres; struggles with debts. *César Birotteau.* First part of *Les Illusions perdues.*

1838   Starts an exploitation of silver mines in Sardinia, which fails.

1839   *Béatrix.* Second part of *Les Illusions perdues. Une Fille d'Eve.*

1840   Failure on the stage of his play *Vautrin.* Founds the *Revue Parisienne* where he attacks Sainte-Beuve and praises Stendhal.

1841   Seriously ill. Groups his writings under the title *La Comédie Humaine.*

1842   *La Rabouilleuse, Albert Savarus.* Urged by his publisher Hetzel, he writes in July his famous "Avant Propos."

1843– Travels to Russia, visits several German cities, stays with
1846   Countess Hanska and her daughter in Dresden, feels his health failing. Accumulates furniture in his Parisian house, where he hopes to settle after his marriage with Mme Hanska.

1848   Dismayed by the February revolution, fails as a candidate to the Constituent Assembly and to the French Academy. Publication of last masterpieces, *La Cousine Bette* and *Le Cousin Pons.*

Chronology

1849– Last trip to the Ukraine. Marries Countess Hanska, March
1850   14. Back in Paris in May. Very ill in July, dies August 21,
       1850. Burial at Père La Chaise cemetery. Resounding speech
       by V. Hugo, "Funérailles de Balzac," published in *Actes et
       Paroles.*

CHAPTER 1

On the Author of
La Comédie Humaine

I   Balzac's Mysterious Personality,
His Family and Times

THANKS to Balzac's extensive correspondence, to the huge and
valuable research accomplished by a number of Balzacians
(Spoelberch de Lovenjoul being the first and still the most
essential), we are very well informed on many events and details of
the author's existence. But any retelling of the struggles, the hopes,
or the loves of Balzac is bound to remain exterior to an understanding of his creative impulse. The working of his imagination is
as mysterious as that of Shakespeare or of Dante. Sources have
been explored in long specialized studies for many of his novels: *La
Recherche de l'Absolu, Eugénie Grandet, Les Illusions perdues.*
They reveal how Balzac's inspiration may have caught fire from occasional readings, and how he molded available material into an
original and personal creation. But the relation between the man's
turbulent, often wretched life, his naïve egotism, his unbounded
capacity for self-delusion, and the novels which he mass-produced,
remains an enigma.

Unlike Benjamin Constant or Stendhal, Balzac did not scrutinize
in private diaries his own moods and his every vacillation. It is in
the fictional, distorted, at times self-pitying and complacent,
portrayals of himself which he composed (in *Louis Lambert,* in the
protagonist of *La Peau de Chagrin* and *Les Illusions perdues*) that
we may catch a more intimate glimpse of him: it is indeed possible
that his actual existence may have been for him less real than the
one of which he dreamed. Behind his exuberance and his poses in
his long epistolary confessions to Eva Hanska and to a number of

other women friends, there remain areas of silence and not a little
secretiveness in the novelist's personality. The gap between the man
and the author is as wide for him as it is for Racine or Proust. The
striking sentence which he penned in a letter to Mme Hanska in
1837, while not devoid of some Byronic pose, is basically justified.
Albert Béguin set it as the epigraph of his book on Balzac: "I am
inexplicable for everybody, for no one possesses the secret of my
life, and I refuse to surrender it to anyone."[1]

A great man, Baudelaire remarked, is not an aerolith. Balzac's
generation counts some of the richest literary talents which ever appeared in Europe. Vigny, Michelet, Hugo, Mérimée, Dumas the
elder, Sainte-Beuve, George Sand, Tocqueville, Delacroix, and
Berlioz were all born within a seven-year span, 1797–1804. Those
years also happen to have been among the most glorious periods of
French history. 1797 saw the victory of Rivoli, the ending of
Bonaparte's whirlwind Italian campaign, soon followed by the
Egyptian expedition. The triumphant general had appointed himself as First Consul in 1799 and his Consulate, which he
transformed in 1804 into the Imperial Régime, was an era of
revitalization of the French economy and of political reconciliation
for the parties. Napoleon, his army, and his court, will often be
conjured up in the pages of *La Comédie Humaine*. Balzac is not
always consistent in his political ideas, although closer to the
monarchists upholding legitimacy. Yet, through the effulgent
memories of the Napoleonic wars often dramatized in his stories,
he is to be counted — almost as much as the royalist Victor Hugo
and the liberal leftist Béranger — among the literary forgers of the
Napoleonic myth.

An indomitable energy, an eagerness to undertake colossal tasks
and to revolutionize painting, music, history, poetry, drama, and
fiction, an impatience with the conventional rules which had long
shackled the arts, characterize those men of superior gifts who were
born around 1800. Very few of them came from the ranks of the
aristocracy. Most of them were born and raised in middle-class
families, with roots in the peasantry. Each of them was driven by
the same question implicitly asked by several of Balzac's ambitious
young men, eager to reap the fruits of the successive French revolu-
tions, "why not I?" In reaching their thirtieth year, those men who
had held their impetuous talent in check for a decade were to witness, if not to provoke, the outburst of Romanticism, which had
long been gathering momentum. The brief revolution of July 1830

appeared to open up unlimited possibilities for them to make a career in politics as well as in literature. A powerful demographic and industrial revolution then shook France. The novelists, Balzac in the forefront of them, were among the first to notice it, to describe it, and to foresee some of its consequences: the rise of criminality and the power of money. Unlike some of his contemporaries who had some income as landed gentry (Lamartine, Vigny, Tocqueville) or held a position in the administration (Stendhal, Mérimée, Michelet), young Balzac realized, as he entered literary life, that he would have to live by his pen. From the outset, he was condemned to what Sainte-Beuve invidiously called "the industrial literature." The miracle is that such a literature, always composed under pressure and often in installments for the diversion of newspaper readers, turned out to be profound, enduring, and frequently artistic.

Balzac's origins were plebeian and provincial. The name of the family was originally Balssa and it came from the southwestern section of France near Albi. The novelist's ebullience and his bragging propensities could be attributed to what he often referred to for his characters as "southern temperament." He seldom alluded to his southern origins or went back to the seat of his paternal family. If he recognized any roots or professed attachment to any place outside of Paris, it was for Touraine, the Rabelaisian province he so lovingly described in *Le Lys dans la Vallée*. From his father, Bernard François Balzac, he may have inherited the robust temperament which enabled him to expend, during his thirty creative years, more energy than most other people in twice as long. He also knew that he owed much to his father's lively conversations on politics, ethics, religion, medicine.

The elder Balzac, after being raised as a peasant boy, read, studied, moved to Paris, like so many of the characters his son was to create. In 1767 he started with a modest position as a lawyer's clerk, but rose to a higher position during the revolution. He worked in military supplies during the Napoleonic years, survived several changes of regime and piled up a sizable investment. He also wrote several small pamphlets on sundry topics, one of them a "Memoir on the outrageous disorder caused by jilted and abandoned girls." Ironically, he was himself, past the age of eighty, accused of being responsible for the pregnancy of just such a girl. He died in 1829, in time to guess the future success of his son as an author. It might be of some significance for the future development of young Balzac to mention here that a brother of Bernard-François, Louis Balssa, was guillotined in Albi in 1819, accused of having murdered a maid he had seduced. Honoré was twenty at the time and must have pondered over the case. Bernard-François had married, in 1797, a Parisian girl from a middle-class family, twenty-two years younger than himself. She was eighteen, attractive, provided with a substantial dowry (which eventually helped pay off some of Honoré's mounting debts). Honoré was the eldest of her four children — and, he often contended, the least loved and the most neglected. The mother was gifted, highly sensitive, moody and touchy, probably not happy in her marriage to an older man, a Voltairian rationalist with pragmatic attitudes to life. She was strongly drawn to esoteric and half-mystical doctrines, such as had swept France in the latter part of the eighteenth century, and it was she who probably introduced Honoré to Swedenborg, Mesmer, Saint-Martin, and other "Illuminists," as they are often called. The novelist of *Seraphita* and of a revealing and strange fragment, *Les Martyrs ignorés,* will repeatedly plead for the occult sciences, much as his mother had done and, perhaps, in unconscious imitation of her. Yet Balzac repeatedly complained, especially when appealing for Mme Hanska's sympathy, of having been denied true maternal love. No doubt inspired by his early sorrows, mothers appear, in Balzac's fiction, irritable and selfish or, in emulation of the unattained ideal of his youth, utterly devoted and self-denying.

Like the hero of his *Louis Lambert,* young Balzac was sent by his parents to the Oratorian College of Vendôme, not far from Tours where his family lived. As a boarder there, he apparently fared no better than Louis Lambert, was often punished for indiscipline, and was weakened by excessive intellectual work. Only twice, during six years of residence at Vendôme, did his mother visit him. He lived all the anguish of a lonely child, nourished by dreams alone and a yearning for freedom and vague conquests. He then went for a year to the Lycée in Tours and, after the fall of Napoleon, transferred to two successive schools in Paris. In 1816 his father found a modest place for him with the lawyer Guyonnet-Merville, who was later immortalized as Derville in *La Comédie.* But the young Balzac, whose imagination had been fired by voracious reading and philosophical speculations, was repelled by the prospects of a law career. Between his fifteenth and twentieth years he had come across Locke, Helvétius, Condillac, perhaps the contemporary Maine de Biran, and, like many young men in the early years of the Restoration, he had been inflamed by the eloquence and glib philosophical generalizations of Victor Cousin.

II *Philosophical Fascinations and First Literary Attempts*

One of the American Balzacian scholars of note, Martin Kanes, has made much of a ten page "Dissertation on Man," composed by the future novelist in 1819 and dealing, in a confused and rather unprofound manner, with metaphysical and linguistic issues that were most likely acquired secondhand. Neither there nor in other essays and fragments in which he speculated on abstract questions (the most notable being a long letter published in the *Revue de Paris* in 1832 on Charles Nodier's article on "Human Palingenesis and Resurrection") did Balzac prove a systematic or original thinker. Had he been such a thinker, his fiction might have been the worse for it, no doubt. Yet he spent several years of intellectual ebullience pondering on the philosophical mysteries that often excite young men. His earliest, and his most turgid, attempts at fiction, in 1821, blend abstract speculation, sentimentality, and melodramatic effects in a work entitled *Sténie ou les Erreurs philosophiques*. From that juvenile intoxication with ideas, Balzac was to retain a lifelong concern with the tantalizing problems of the relations between man's physical well-being and the exertions of thought, between matter, mind, and the secret springs of willpower and energy. He soon realized that, if he were to make his mark in the world of letters, he must give life to his abstract speculations with flesh and blood characters. He made one infelicitous attempt at tragedy on the then timely subject of Cromwell. But the gift for expressing himself in verse eluded that most dramatic of novelists, and Balzac failed in almost all his ventures on the stage — much as did Flaubert, the Goncourts, and Zola.

Honoré's parents had decided they would accede, for a time at least, to his eager desire to write. They then lived near Melun at Villeparisis, where their son often came to visit. They rented for him at a pittance a wretched garret near the Bastille in Paris, in the Faubourg Saint-Antoine. This was often recalled by the novelist, especially in the first page of his strange and powerful story "Facino Cane," (1836). All those years in Rue Lesdiguières will miraculously spring to life in his work, the unheated and shabby room where visions had magically risen from his imagination and made him envisage the conquest of the world through his pen — much as Napoleon had done with his sword, he was to say. He ate little and irregularly in those days, kept awake with numerous cups of coffee, and covered reams of paper, struggling to give shape and substance to his dreams of glory. Sometime he would take a stroll at night and vicariously live the life of the men and women along the road, who spoke softly of their needs and their sorrows. "To break away from one's habits, to become another person through the intoxication of one's moral powers," he wrote to his sister in November 1819, "and play that game at will, such was my pastime." Amidst the misery and the loneliness of those years, a sense of freedom had also reigned and dreams had shattered the walls of ugliness and despair. He had "the Nouvelle Héloise for a mistress, La Fontaine as a friend, Boileau as a judge and the Père Lachaise cemetery to stroll in."[2]

III   *A Lasting Love and Other Friends*

When Honoré first met Laure de Berny, a friend of the family then living in Villeparisis, he was twenty-two years old — and she twenty-two years older. A deep friendship between them soon developed into a love composed of trust and admiration, of encouragement and devotion. Laure de Berny was perhaps the first person to discern the future novelist in the eager young man and to see that his passionate fantasy contained the germ of greatness. She was the mother of ten children, and the young Balzac had in fact been called to tutor one of them. Her life with her difficult husband — possibly a source for M. de Mortsauf in *Le Lys dans ia Vallée,* and she herself the model for Henriette — must not always have been pleasant. Honoré's fervor must have been like the irruption of sunshine upon her world. He was ardent, pressing in his entreaties, naïve and awkward, profuse with declarations of love. After almost a year's siege, she surrendered in the summer of 1822. Their liaison lasted for some eight years, inevitably with a few infidelities on the part of the young man. She continued to be a source of inspiration, of warmth and assistance until her death in 1836, and remained to the end his "dilecta." Her reward was in watching his early success as a novelist and in seeing her faith in his genius confirmed. Balzac's indebtedness to her was to a degree acquitted by the tender portraits he created for some of his heroines, those who, inspired by his "dilecta," gave unstintingly with love and understanding: Pauline in *La Peau de Chagrin,* Henriette in *Le Lys,* Mme Claes of *La Recherche de l'Absolu,* and perhaps even Mme Hulot of *La Cousine Bette.*

Before his thirtieth year, Balzac had encountered two other women who were to exert a degree of influence on his life. The first, Zulma Carraud, had been a school friend of his sister; she later married an artillery officer who had been in Napoleon's army and even suffered as a prisoner of the English. From him Balzac heard tales of Napoleonic deeds and wars; from her he received not only devotion and comfort, but the intelligent friendship that does not shun criticism. Zulma considered herself too ugly to have any lasting romantic claim upon Balzac, and she gently rebuked him on that score. "If I had had other looks ('une autre enveloppe')," she wrote to him on November 28, 1832, "yes, I would have been the woman made for you: I would have loved you very much."[3] The novelist may have had her in mind when he sketched a plot around "the loves of an ugly woman." The project was given up, although something of it was passed on, in satirical form, to his splendid *La Vieille Fille* a few years later. Zulma's friendship was, along with that of Laure de Berny, one of the most valuable that Balzac was to receive in his life. He often appealed to her and sought refuge in her house in Angoulême.

The third woman to play a role in his existence was the Duchess of Abrantès. They were probably first drawn to each other in the late 1820s when Balzac worked as a kind of literary hack in sketching semifictional memoirs. He had then had occasion to meet Laure Abrantès, the widow of one of Napoleon's generals, Junot. He helped her write her memoirs and was fascinated by a woman who had approached Napoleon himself. She was some fifteen years older than Honoré, but this must have been an asset with the young writer still pursuing the fleeting image of a mistress-mother-companion. It is from this Laure that Balzac gathered so many entertaining anecdotes on the life of the Imperial court, and by her that he was introduced to the salons of Imperial nobility, whose ebullience and assertive aspirations were to be immortalized in the pages of *La Comédie.*

Balzac's amorous liaisons were numerous and varied. Much has been made of his virile energy, but the truth may be found more in his sentimental need for woman's companionship than in his erotic desires. Despite his unprepossessing appearance — he was small,

with disproportionately short legs beneath a round body, a huge
head, and gaps in his teeth — and despite his rather coarse
manners, he often proved of irresistible charm to women. He
understood them and knew how to encourage their confidence,
how to appeal to their tenderness and elicit their admiration. He
recognized the magic resonance that words could evoke in a
woman's heart and the unavowed yearning for poetry in their lives.
"Artists alone are worthy of women," he wrote, "because they
have a little of women in themselves."[4] Balzac realized that the
man of letters he had most admired in his youth, Walter Scott, had
never gone beyond the most conventional portrayal of womankind,
and to this he attributed the failure of that English novelist. Love
remained in Balzac's life an undisguised and romantic longing for
understanding, to be cherished against the phantoms of loneliness.

IV   *The Slow Emergence of the Novelist*

While he was proceeding with his sentimental education and
courting passion, Balzac was at the same time frantically trying to
earn money and endeavoring to pave the road to future literary
success. The indiscriminate philosophical reading he had been
absorbing, chiefly through manuals, was drawn into two series,
"Notes on philosophy and religion" and "Notes on the im-
mortality of the soul." They were earnest but little more than
elementary reflections on books borrowed from the Arsenal
library. The notion that the qualities of the mind are a function of
the brain or, at any rate, are conditioned by it, was then a common-
place. It had been inherited from late-eighteenth-century, so-called
"materialist" thinkers and was current in Cabanis and Bichat,
famous medical men of 1800–1820. To these ill-digested
philosophical readings, which the novelist was later to rethink and
enliven with a personal and passionate touch, young Honoré added
an equally avid perusal of novels translated from the English.
Those were the works of Maturin, Sterne, Walter Scott, and
Fenimore Cooper. Later he devoured Byron, like all cultured
French men of the 1830s, and he was impressed with Otway's
tragedy of 1682, *Venice preserved,* to which he was repeatedly to al-
lude in his fiction.

During the years 1819–1824, Balzac composed a number of
crude, hasty novels. The purpose was twofold, to earn money — in
which he did not succeed — and to gain competence in the art of

writing. Those early novels were not signed with his real name. Balzac was not proud of them and he preferred to hide the identity of their author under pseudonyms such as Horace de Saint-Aubyn or Lord R'hoone. He later allowed some of them to be reprinted, or he borrowed passages from them, but on the whole they must be seen as his apprenticeship in writing rather than accomplished works. They would receive no attention today if critics were not eager to discern even in the earliest compositions glimpses of the future genius. Four Balzacian scholars in particular have studied those crude melodramatic stories with more care than they probably deserve, attempting to see the genesis of a great writer through the study of his earliest literary attempts — in tales that blend ambitious philosophical generalities and sentimental developments with conventional horror themes, incest, undertones of eroticism, murder. Those scholars, whose books are listed in our bibliography, are P. Barbéris, M. Bardèche, B. Guyon, and A. Prioult.

Sténie ou les Erreurs philosophiques was composed between 1819 and 1820, and it is placed at the same time. The familiar contention that the author of *Les Chouans* began with the historical novel, "à la Walter Scott," could thus be considered unjustified. This earlier work is, in fact, closer to the epistolary fiction of Richardson and Rousseau. The theme of two contrasting moralities — one passionate and demanding, the other supportive and accepting — will later be taken up in *Mémoires de deux jeunes Mariées,* without, however, the copious tears and moans, the desperate gestures and overdramatization that fill the pages of *Sténie.* A few developments on the uncontrolled power of passion will perhaps furnish the model for the events in *Louis Lambert,* but this resemblance too may be contestable.

Of approximately the same period (1820), *Falthurne* owes more to Byron's *Corsair* and *Lara* and to the English "black" novel than to either Richardson or Scott. It is in a tradition that enjoyed great popularity in Paris around 1825, after the appearance of Brillat-Savarin's manual of gastronomy. There were several other volumes written in melodramatic tones with easy emotional appeal for the common reader, some of them done in collaboration with two other writers of uncertain qualifications, Etienne Arago and Poitevin de l'Egreville. *L'Héritière de Birague, Jean-Louis ou la Fille trouvée, Clotilde de Lusignan ou le beau Juif, Le Vicaire des Ardennes* are some of the titles. *Le Centenaire ou les deux*

Berengheld is somewhat more notable, with a complicated story involving the secret of eternal life through a periodically recurring sacrifice of a human life. *Annette et le Criminel* and *Wann-Chlore* are perhaps the first attempts at the psychological novel and the last youthful works of Balzac. They close the protracted period of apprenticeship and usher the way to worthier endeavors.

In 1827 appeared *La Physiologie du Mariage,* a cynical, entertaining, and devastating quasi-study on the relation and behavior of couples. It received considerable acclaim and was later retained among the works published under the name of "Balzac." The 1829 version is replete with anecdotes, spicy remarks, and Rabelaisian satire, skillfully presented as observations written by a young bachelor, with a warning in the frontispiece, "Ladies do not enter here." Inevitably, they rushed to buy the book.

The literary glory of which young Honoré had dreamed seemed, meanwhile, distressingly elusive. If writers with secure reputations for excellence — Stendhal or Lamartine among his elders, Vigny or Hugo among those of his age group — ever heard of him, it was, surely, as a hack writer not deserving of much attention. In 1826 Balzac, somewhat discouraged by literary prospects and led by rash advisers and a publisher, Urbain Canel, undertook to launch on the market new editions of French classics: Molière, La Fontaine. The prefaces he himself wrote to those editions were devoid of originality and the venture proved a financial failure, resulting in bankruptcy. Instead of hitting upon the gold mine he had envisaged, Balzac ran into heavy debts. He then conceived the even more rash scheme of buying a printing press and a foundry, which he would run himself. He never lacked inventiveness as a man of affairs, but the necessary practical sense eluded him. By temperament he eschewed all attention to minute details, all prudence and restraint, and, probably, also the wily lack of scruples that might have given him success. The debts he incurred at this time were long to weigh upon his career. He was reduced to borrowing both from Mme de Berny and from his mother. But these experiences in the domain of business were otherwise profitable for him. He was later able to build stories that rested upon a solid knowledge of the world of trade and the realization of the ascendancy of money in post-Napoleonic France. His disastrous financial ventures thus managed to give him a sense for the concrete that had until then been deficient in him — a first inkling of the reality that would eventually be transmitted to his artistic production.

Cured of his money making schemes, Balzac came back to the one thing with which he was most familiar and that had first made him envision paths of glory. Writing would from now on be his constant companion and consuming passion — albeit in the name of money, often, and through the sheer necessity to survive. The immense vogue then enjoyed by Walter Scott and the historical novel was a stimulus for writing what became the first volume of *La Comédie Humaine, Le dernier Chouan,* later called simply *Les Chouans.* It sold poorly, but it impressed the literary circles. Balzac was turning for the first time to reality, even if it was the reality of 1799. Still disguised, but very much at the base of it, are the lessons learned from his business ventures. These will later bear distinctive fruits with the portrayal of David Séchard, a printer and infelicitous inventor in *Les Illusions perdues,* or with the bankruptcy of César Birotteau. *Les Chouans,* while not dealing with business, touches upon the basic realities of war — not only those composites of idealism, sentiment, and the quest for freedom, but those material necessities which dominate the world of men.

Les Chouans won Balzac his first entry into the literature of the new age. He had, until then, been aloof from the Romantic movement that was electrifying the Parisian world of letters. Stendhal's manifesto on *Racine et Shakespeare* had appeared in 1823 and 1825, and Hugo's preface to *Cromwell* in 1827. In an "avant propos" to *Le Gar* (the initial title), then in a second preface to *Le dernier Chouan* in 1829, Balzac asserts his claim to being a social moralist and a philosopher of history, eager to place the history of his country within the reach of all. "Today the great lessons unrolled in the pages of history must become popular," he wrote. Like the young liberals of the time — Augustin Thierry, Guizot, Thiers, Mignet — Balzac wanted to portray the spirit of an age defined by the last years of the revolution and the advent of the Consulate. With poetic irony, he attempted to be fair to the two fiercely opposing sides, that of the "Whites" or Royalist fanatics, and that of the "Blues" or new Republicans. But his admiration at this time is still pronouncedly in favor of the liberals; the villains that emerge are the reactionary Church exploiting the superstitious fears of the poor, and the fanatic aristocrats impeding progress. The figure of Marie de Verneuil — a woman who vindicates her turbulent past and acquires heroic dimensions through the purity and exaltation of her love for the leader of the Chouans — and Major Hulot — who will later reappear as Marshall and elder

brother of the notorious Baron Hulot in *La Cousine Bette* — are
the first powerful characters yet drawn by the novelist.
While the events described in the novel are historically true, the
characters are fictitious. Love and history are blended with the
wilderness of Britanny and its proud people, devoted to freedom
and the claim of their land. The influence of Walter Scott is still
present, but Balzac might have been inspired by Lady Morgan and
her detailed descriptions of Ireland also. The action is synchronized
to the necessities of the place, and nature becomes a layout, a stage
upon which battles, ambushes, and betrayals are unfolded. For the
first time, perhaps, action is visible, dictated by an inner logic and
placed in a natural setting. Details are amassed leading in crescendo
to the "dénouement" at the end. Balzac would not again recapture
the highly romantic exaltation that stands at the center of the plot
in *Les Chouans;* nor would he — with the possible exception of
Catherine de Médicis composed between 1830 and 1841 in three
separate parts, and not deserving a place among his more notable
works — come back to the historical novel. *Les Chouans,* with its
underlying thesis praising the sovereign who encouraged the St.
Bartholomew massacre, and denouncing the Reformation as a
source of disunity anticipating the revolution, is hardly a popular
novel with modern readers. While the novelist was to express his
satisfaction with it years later and to incorporate it in *La Comédie,*
it must perhaps be seen not as the first work of his "opus
magnum" but rather as the last of his youth.

CHAPTER 2

The Philosophical Novels

I *The Flowering of a New Maturity*

A T thirty-one, in the year 1830–31, Balzac reached miraculously
full creative maturity. All the diverse and often contradictory
ideas that had so long been fermenting in his mind, the stylistic ap-
proaches and philosophical preoccupations that had been crowding
his literary production, suddenly seemed to reach a climacteric
point. The catalyst in this may have been outside events helping the
novelist establish clearer alliances, both politically and ethically.

Balzac did not witness the "three glorious days" that toppled the
Bourbon monarchy. He thought at first that a new era would now
start, that new ways would be open for an impatient French youth
that had merely been marking time during the Restoration period.
But from the expectations that were suddenly revived and
nourished with old idealism and flights of fantasy, only a new set of
tensions and disappointments arose. A mere year after the "Liberty
on the barricades," the participants of the July uprising are seen by
Balzac as robbed of their aim. Their revolution appears empty and
a cruel irony in the course of events. His political views, which had
never been totally clear, now gain a certain vigor, encouraged by a
new conservatism and inspired by the aristocrats whom the novelist
has begun to frequent. Vigor will not mean clarity all the time,
however, and even in *Le Médecin de Campagne* three years later,
offered as an expression of political philosophy, his views would be
far from definite.

After *Les Chouans* and a rapidly acquired fame, Balzac began to
write, early in 1830, a number of short stories. They appeared in
the recently created *Revue de Paris,* in the *Revue des deux Mondes,*
and in a number of weeklies or daily papers. The novelist then as-

sociated with Henri Monnier, a writer and caricaturist, with
Eugène Lamy, an artist, with Delacroix, who became a close
friend, Horace Vernet, a painter, Eugène Sue, and the composer
Rossini. Along with Théophile Gautier, Gérard de Nerval, and
other boisterous young artists, Balzac was present at the first
performance of *Hernani* in February 1830. Yet soon after, he
flayed the romantic drama as preposterous, unconvincing, and
unoriginal. His own brand of romantic imagination was to be fed
through other sources. The tales of Hoffmann were then enjoying a
great vogue in Paris, and it is to them that are due both the
elements of the fantastic and the first attempts at establishing
correspondences between different arts and multiple sensitivities.
"L'Elixir de longue Vie" and *La Peau de Chagrin* borrowed
themes and tone from the German storyteller. This was the time
when Lamartine, Hugo, young Musset, Gautier, were pouring
volumes of verses on an ecstatic public.

Literary salons were flourishing — those of Baron Gérard, of
Delphine Gay (soon to become Mme de Girardin) were frequented
by Balzac; but he remained, on the whole, indifferent to poetry and
never fully identified with the Romantics. Unlike some of them, he
did not turn away from the classics. In fact, next to Rabelais, who
inspired his *Contes drolatiques* begun at this time, the novelist
claims more kinship with Molière than with any of his
contemporaries. Long before he created Mme Marneffe of *La
Cousine Bette,* he pondered about the possibilities of a female
Tartuffe, and all through his work we see traces of that great
Classicist's studies of man's foibles and passions. Balzac's most
romantic trait, in those early months of the July Monarchy, was his
fascination with symbols and myths, and his quest for evidence of
the possible action of the supernatural upon daily life. Goethe's
Faust, translated in part by Nerval in 1828, and Byron's *Manfred,*
Delacroix's lithographs of Faust and Hamlet later, had greater
impact upon his artistic development than all the "Cénacles" of the
time. Now fully in possession of his resources as a philosophical
novelist, Balzac aimed at rivaling the greatest European dramatist
with the publication of *La Peau de Chagrin* and *Louis Lambert.*

II   La Peau de Chagrin

The hero of that symbolic and fantastic tale ranks among the
Romantic characters afflicted with the "mal du siècle" or disease

of the century; in them rage conflicting forces that impede both fulfillment and abjuration of desires, with ensuing weariness or death. Balzac's Raphael embodies many of the author's dreams during his long period of hectic and chaotic activity at the beginning of his career. He is a dreamer and a gambler, an audacious challenger of the mysterious order imposed upon events. Caught within the passion of the moment at hand, blind to the fatality of time passing, Raphael de Valentin defies an all-knowing creator delving in infinity and an eternal present. We learn next to nothing about his past, his family, his studies, the repeated frustrations which have plunged him into the trough of despair. Introduced in the autumn of 1829, the story opens as he enters a gambling house in the Palais Royal. Absentmindedly he had forgotten to check his shabby hat with the pale-faced, crouched old man behind the counter. Are death and fate always in wait? What is the recondite meaning of those rites and rules that transform a gambling hall into a capsule of reality removed from all other? The visitor must abdicate his individuality upon entering, much as Sartre's three captives of a closed hell must stare at the unvarying dimensions of their windowless room.

At once, instead of proceeding with a straight narrative, the author weaves didactic but colorful and gripping comments on the enigmatic significance of gambling. He describes with a few masterful touches the dingy room, the ominous silence, and the expressionless faces of the gamblers already present, who gaze with surprise at the obviously inexperienced newcomer. They have the intent but curiously detached appearance of onlookers of an executioner at work, anticipating impassively the cutting of a head. Those cold and "blasés" gamblers feel almost pity for the tense and silent novice and the aura of tragedy that seems to hover upon his features. He utters not a word, looks at no one, remains unperturbed as his last coin is swept away by the ivory rod. His next move will inevitably be suicide. Balzac, always a master of the technique of digression, shares with the reader his reflections on suicide, a subject that haunted many Romantics pondering on the fate of *Werther, René, Hamlet*. Raphael strolls along the quays and on the bridges of the Seine, gazes at the murky waters, distributes a few coins found in his pocket to some beggars who promise, in return, to pray for his long life. A longing glance at a young lady by an art shop is his farewell to womankind. All thoughts of love, elegance, wealth have been left behind. Only an hour of waiting is

left before night falls and the dark river below engulfs him in end-
less silence. He enters an antique shop nearby to while away the last
fleeting moments. Like a character from the *Arabian Nights,* he is dazzled by the
remnants of all civilizations heaped up in the curiosity shop. The
mythical dimension of the novel, transfigured into an epic, is
revealed here. Raphael is both fascinated and repelled with those
debris of the past, of culture and art displayed in all their vanity.
The visitor is taken to the centenarian, a wizened man who, rising
from poverty, has traveled through continents, purchased all those
treasures, and presides over that strange assortment with "the quiet
lucidity of a God who sees everything or the proud strength of a
man who has seen all" (1. 32). At a hundred and two, he knows
and reveals to the bewildered stranger the secret of human life.
Man's vitality is drained through two forces: desire, which inflames
him, and power, which can destroy him. Knowledge alone gives the
necessary peace. The old antiquarian has survived by watching
from afar the battles of life, skirting all excesses, maintaining both
senses and emotions under control, transforming all loves, ambitions, sorrows into impersonal ideas. This then should be the lesson, to avoid all contact with the pitfalls of passion and to remain
forever impervious to the appeals of the senses.

Raphael is understandably unconvinced by the sermon. He has
caught sight of a shagreen (or wild ass's skin) behind a glass case.
Whoever accepts the gift of that talisman, he learns, will have all
wishes at once fulfilled. But each time, with the granting of every
desire, the skin will shrink accordingly. As it is reduced to naught,
the owner's life will reach its end. Raphael does not confront a
Mephistophelian pact that will claim his soul at the end. He deals
merely with the dimensions of his own existence, visibly
corresponding from that moment on to the withering magic skin.
No thought of the future injects a moment's hesitation in his deci-
sion; he grabs the deceptive talisman and joyfully saunters along
the banks of the river, all temptation of suicide relinquished to the
past.

The element of the fantastic appears in the story as a blend of
empirical reality with man's hopes and dreams. Precise descriptions
of surroundings and of people's faces are expertly fused with vague
wishes and yearnings. It seems natural that Raphael should hit
upon his friends who were searching for him. His first wish, as he
leaves the antique shop in a state of daze, is for a banquet at which

he would entertain them. They all repair to their Walpurgis night, reveling in sensuous pleasure and abundance. Balzac describes their orgy: choice food, drink, exotic delicacies, intermingled with sparkling conversation on philosophy, politics, love. Courtesans are present: Aquilina, named after Thomas Otway's heroine in *Venice Preserved,* and Euphrasia, condemned to a life of pleasure, as the novelist puts it, but proud of living more intensely in one day than respectable housewives in ten years. Through them, the courtesan appears as a magnified force that gathers society under its spell and reigns upon it.

Excited by the nearness of beautiful women, by drink, and by the superhuman power just acquired, Raphael now relates the story of his youth, his long submission to rigid paternal authority, his first temptation with gambling, the misery and eventual death he brought to his father through his debauchery. He longed for an ideal woman who would cherish and understand him, but women shunned his earnest and thoughtful nature. Feeling doomed to loneliness and impecuniousness, he had rented a garret on the left bank, where he meditated, dreamed, wrote, still yearning for the feminine presence that would one day console him. He had sketched a lengthy treatise on willpower — the same which Balzac will soon ascribe to Raphael's double, Louis Lambert. The landlady's daughter, Pauline, almost a child, had offered a pale ray of comfort to his dejected life, discreetly helping him with his room and occasionally adding something to his skimpy meals. Raphael repaid her kindness by giving her a few lessons. He respected her gentle and affectionate nature. But his dream remained obstinately linked to a different image, that of an aristocratic woman, haughty, heartless perhaps, a siren beckoning from afar, mysterious and alluring. Rastignac had been instrumental in his meeting Foedora and luring him into a more glamorous existence. Foedora, that queen of salons sought by the wealthiest aristocrats of France, had spurned all advances, remaining elusively distant and inaccessible. The young man's imagination had caught fire and he became obsessed by her.

As he continues telling his story, Raphael relates that Foedora's appearance was that of an idol among idolaters. Scientists, writers, statesmen, noblemen were at her feet, paying homage and offering their hearts. She toyed with them all but remained unconquerable. Raphael had thought her worthy of listening to his theories and began to expound on the nature of ideas being living organisms, invisible and incorporeal, but controlling our destinies. Descartes, Diderot, Napoleon had been illustrations of the incontrovertible power of ideas. The young man was at his most brilliant and Foedora had been fascinated, almost amorous, but her body remained frigid. Raphael, on the other hand, was conquered, victim of his own imagination and the desire to attain the unattainable. With no money, no decent apparel, no carriage of his own, he had then been swept by the fire of ambition; he would win Foedora or die.

One evening, invited to her mansion after the theater, he was flustered by her unambiguous warning: she would surrender to nobody's love. He had retorted with scathing remarks but she had refused even to feel hurt. Gloomily, he had gone back to his room to find the affectionate and devoted Pauline. But Foedora asked him back and he was powerless to resist. Again, he fell under her sway and spent his last "sou." Pauline offered to go and pawn his scant possessions for him, and the gold coins thus acquired took him back to Foedora. He hid in her room as she prepared for her night's sleep — a lunar and cold beauty sliding among chaste sheets. She still refused him and their talks soon resembled acid repartees. Their verbal duels are masterpieces of wit from which a full characterization of the two antagonists emerges. Pascal in his *Provinciales* and Voltaire had never achieved any more virtuoso mastery of irony. Raphael went home, worn out and seething with anger. Pauline's gentle devotion could not soothe him. He met once again his evil genie, Rastignac, who derided the notion of suicide: every young man has thought of it three or four times before the age of thirty; few have done it. All the author's didactic intrusions here do not diminish the tragic power of the scene, where desire and the yearnings of the senses acquire the ominous weight of a fatality.

The night of orgy is nearing its end. Raphael, in possession of the talisman, is ready to wreak his revenge on life. Extravagance becomes his domain, lavishness the easy tool of conquest; all wishes and cravings of the restless age in which he lives are summed up and held victoriously within reach. Foedora could be his, but he scorns what is facile; he aims at rarefied peaks, but the size of the skin, worn by his thirst for life and adventure, shrinks: "only the last panel of the triptych, or death agony," remains. Raphael, who soon becomes an immensely wealthy marquis, begins to lead a secluded life, meticulously banishing all opportunities that could lead him to desire. His gloomy existence, governed by fear, is graphically described by his faithful servant to all would-be visitors. Everything is arranged so that any wish of the master may be anticipated. His ascetic life resembles that of an automaton, carefully following a prescribed path, heedful not to deviate into the realm of emotions and sensations. "To him, the shagreen skin was like a tiger, with which he had to live without awaking its ferociousness" (9. 163). He meets the aged antique dealer to whom he owed the talisman; in anger, he allows himself the luxury of a wish: that the centenarian enter upon a life of pleasure. True to the fatal power of the skin, the old man becomes indeed one of the pursuers of Euphrasia and one hour of love is suddenly worth to him more than a whole life of prudent economy of his vital force.

Raphael meantime has endeavored to become what the old man had been, indifferent to human passions and removed from life's dilemmas. The sight of Foedora, at a theatrical celebration one evening, is but a meaningless vision to him. Aquilina, Rastignac, the banker Taillefer, float by without shaking him from his torpor. Amidst them, however, suddenly appears Pauline, richly dressed and resplendent; his old tenderness immediately grows into rapturous love. The skin dwindles into microscopic size, indicating that only two months of life are left. Thrown into a well, the talisman is rescued by the gardener and brought back to its master. The ineluctable fatality of its presence weighs against the intervention of men of science. The zoologist, the physicist, and the chemist that are visited talk at length but to no avail: all the science of the three grotesque and Rabelaisian figures is in vain. Four more doctors are called to the death bed, so that the process of Raphael's decline may at least be understood. They dissert in grave and solemn disagreement, like Molière's medical specialists; a trip to Aix Les Bains is their final suggestion. Unwanted by the guests there, the dying man's presence throws a chill and an ominous warning. Provoked by one of the guests who wishes him to leave, Raphael fights a duel. His Pyrrhic victory reduces the skin to the size of an oak leaf.

The setting of another resort in the Auvergne, where the hero repairs, is idyllic. Raphael seems rejuvenated for a brief while by the simplicity of agrarian life amidst contented peasants. But the pity he discovers in people's eyes awakens his pride, and he returns to Paris. He will see no one, not even Pauline. Still, his vegetative and drugged sleep is interrupted by a magnificent banquet his servants and doctors had contrived as a present for him. The glitter, the fragrance, the presence of beautiful women, arouse a faint desire in Raphael. Pauline appears as a radiant angel, smiling and dressed in white, in the room where the dying young man has repaired. Under his pillow, he feels the skin, now shrunk to a periwinkle petal. Pauline, convinced that her death would bring him peace, tries to kill herself. In a supreme gesture, he rises from his couch and rushes frantically to her. This last act brings his final collapse.

The epilogue of the story is a little awkward. Balzac, in four long pages, stresses the allegorical meaning of his tale. Pauline is a lovely illusion, "a fanciful creation of mists and breeze" over the Loire valley. Foedora is everywhere at the Paris parties. She is "society." Earlier in the tale, the author had formulated the meaning of his mythical novel more cogently: the possession of power does not automatically grant the knowledge of its use. "Power leaves us such as we are and bestows stature only on those who already have it" (9. 151).

III   *The "Skin" Is the Author's Talisman*

With *La Peau de Chagrin* completed soon after his thirtieth year, Balzac achieved a masterpiece which seized readers in France and elsewhere on the continent by storm. A carping critic could easily single out several features of the book for blame. Except for *Madame Bovary* (and even for that novel the point can be contested), the notion of perfection, implying faultlessness and impeccable structure, is out of place in the criticism of fiction. There is but one word to sum up the potent effect of this novel upon its readers: a vitality which assumes magnetic force. From the very first pages, we are seized by the appearance, the gestures, the thoughts of Raphael. The language is rich and sparkles with flamboyance: conciseness never was Balzac's aim, nor was restraint. The novelist accumulates details, multiplies touches of color, plays with hyperboles, and he obviously enjoys throwing his fireworks here and there, inserting at times long monologues. He writes with gusto, varies the tone of his narrative, passing from tragic seriousness and an aura of forebodings, to ironical caricature. With this novel, Balzac first imposes upon his readers his vision of Paris, with all its glitter, ferment, and temptations. Squalid streets and dark bridges are juxtaposed to brilliant halls

Pierrette, and other stories. The device occasionally strains credibility, as Percy Lubbock pointed out.[15] References to earlier productions are at times crudely inserted between brackets, dismaying perhaps the reader who must quickly establish links in his memory, or run to an index in order to clarify the point. Even admirers of Balzac, such as François Mauriac, have not felt happy with being chained to the same characters through so many volumes.

Still, the advantages gained by Balzac from his device are many and they have gained him the admiration of later novelists, such as Proust, Butor, Marceau. Triumphantly, he won his rash wager against all odds. He could endow his characters with a past and with a quality of density seldom possessed even by those of the greatest novelists. He was able to spare painstaking expositions on past life, education, or earlier loves of Marsay or Rastignac, Diane de Maufrigneuse or Mme d'Espard. And he succeeded in surrounding his personages with a thick layer of mystery, even when their social circles, their professions, their ways of life were similar. None of Balzac's military men, none of his convicts or police inspectors, few even of his courtesans are quite alike. All novelists must resort to some assumptions which we must be ready to grant them, just as we do not question the rules of a game. Those of Balzac do not, after all, arouse our resistance, not even in *Ferragus,* "La Fille aux Yeux d'Or," *Splendeurs et Misères,* any more than might those of Dickens, Zola, or Tolstoy. The number of Balzacian characters who, in E. M. Forster's terminology, are more round than flat remains unequaled.

CHAPTER 13

Balzac's Fame and Posterity

I The Resurgence of Balzac Scholarship

AN adequate survey of the reception of Balzac's works, first by his contemporaries, then by the second half of the nineteenth century, in France and outside France, would need the collective research of many scholars and the printing of several volumes. A detailed and balanced work, covering the vicissitudes and the slow growth of Balzac's reputation in France from 1850 to 1900, has been published by a British scholar, David Bellos;[1] but the highest point of Balzac's fortune with novelists, critics, and the public at large was reached later, around 1950, when the centenary of his death was celebrated in several countries. On no other writer has such a mass of first-rate biographical and critical studies been accumulated in the twenty-five years since then, 1950–1975: admiration, fascination, and even affection, are the dominant moods in the volumes that appeared, even in those written by impartial and austere scholars.

Posterity finds it hard to understand why and how Balzac's contemporaries in the critical profession remained obstinately blind to his originality and kept on ranking him more or less on the same level as Eugène Sue, Paul de Kock, Charles de Bernard, and even more obscure authors of lurid tales. The personality of Balzac the man, often boastful, vulgar, querulous, quick to engage in polemics and to start lawsuits, may account for it in part. Balzac eventually quarreled with influential critics, Jules Janin, Henri de Latouche, Philarète Chasles; he spoke acidly of George Sand, Victor Hugo, derided Sainte-Beuve's style with perspicacious humor, and played down his novel and bulky, erudite *Port-Royal.* Still the perfidious and obtuse articles written by Sainte-Beuve on

158

Balzac's novels rank among the worst lapses of judgment and taste committed by a critic with claims to discernment. But we know that Sainte-Beuve regularly failed to understand his contemporaries.

The attacks or the reservations which greeted Balzac's novels during the author's lifetime seldom rested on literary analysis. His critics, Sainte-Beuve at their head, blamed him as a provider of "industrial literature," a fiction which was mass-produced, hastily written, and condescended to coarse effects. His manipulation of everyday reality was judged to reach systematic falsification and to amount to an insult to the reader. Above all, Balzac was suspected of aiming at female audiences and of attempting to win that portion of the public which craved for distorted pictures of passion and for cheap sentimentality. In the last resort, the resistance to Balzac, in the very persons who eagerly bought his books and in writers who envied his fecundity and his success, stemmed from moral prejudices. The novelist repeatedly endeavored to prove (even with elaborate counting of his good characters outnumbering the bad ones, as in his preface to *Le Père Goriot*) that the lesson to be derived from his novels was not immoral. But even in his final estimate of the novelist after his death, Sainte-Beuve did not relent in his hostility. No one, except Hugo who had had the courage to vote for Balzac when the latter was a candidate to the French Academy, seems to have realized that the author of *La Comédie* towered above his contemporaries.

II *Balzac the Revolutionary Writer*

Hugo was not exactly the first to proclaim that Balzac belonged "to the strong race of revolutionary writers," as he said in his eloquent speech at Balzac's grave on August 21, 1850. A leftist journalist and historian, Taxile Delord, had just written that, even when they profess monarchist and Catholic views, "all the vigorous minds of today, whether they are aware of it or not, are working for the Revolution."[2] But the fame of Hugo and the ardent tone of his oration gave wide publicity to that assertion. Balzac, on the other hand, had repeatedly stated his conservative opinions and defined himself a supporter of monarchy and of Catholicism, giving thus some embarrassment to his severest critics, who were in majority royalists and Catholics. The novelist Barbey d'Aurevilly (1808–1889) was one of the first to acclaim Balzac, in an article in *Le Pays* in 1864, as the greatest writer of the century and as a

Catholic. The same assertion will be repeated often by an admirer of Barbey d'Aurevilly and one of the most ardent worshippers of Balzac, Paul Bourget, in the last two decades of the nineteenth century. Since literary criticism in France seldom divorces itself from politics, for three quarters of a century after his death Balzac was to be claimed by conservatives as defender of order, hierachy, and tradition.

Karl Marx's admiration for Balzac's study of the peasantry in his unfinished novel *Les Paysans,* his oft mentioned regret that he had not had the time to write a book on Balzac as a critic of the bourgeoisie, and Friedrich Engels's even warmer admiration for Balzac as a social critic and a denouncer of capitalism, failed to find echoes among the writers of the left. A gifted left-wing journalist, Julien Lemer, in 1892, magnified Balzac as a thinker and as a reformer. Two much more important authors had preceded and inspired the obscure Lemer: the "insurgé" or born protester Jules Vallès, and Emile Zola. Vallès ranked Balzac above all other French novelists, but he dreaded the impact on the young of those heroes, restrained by no scruple and fiercely ambitious, who rushed to conquer Paris and seize political and financial power. The gist of a lecture which he delivered in January 1865 was that, despite his will to be royalist, a Catholic, and an advocate of authority, "Balzac was a great revolutionary."[3] The same partisan view was upheld by Zola. He contradicted himself on Balzac, as on many other authors, but in his early years, during the Second Empire, profoundly impressed by Taine, Zola had seen Balzac as crushing all other writers, Hugo included, by his gigantic genius. In 1869, he claimed that, whatever his intentions and delusions about the political philosophy latent in his fiction, Balzac always remained "the son of a former valet," denouncing the nobility as decadent and showing the people as rightfully called upon to displace and replace their former masters. He concluded by saying that a "broad revolutionary breath" animated his work as a whole.[4]

III *Epoch-making Essay by Taine:*
Balzac as a Visionary

The most important critical piece written on Balzac during the second half of the nineteenth century, and one which has remained challenging to this day, is the long article by Hippolyte Taine.[5]

Many of the views made popular today on Balzac as a visionary and on the power of his imagination recreating reality were formulated in Taine's essay, long before they were taken up by other admirers of Balzac from Baudelaire to Béguin. Little was known of the details of Balzac's life then and few of his splendid letters were available. Still, without prying into the less savory aspects of an author's private existence as Sainte-Beuve was fond of doing, Taine referred some of Balzac's obsessions — such as the power of money in the modern world — to the novelist's debts and business failures. Like George Sand and many earlier dramatists and novelists, from Lope de Vega to Dostoevsky, Balzac probably needed to be unhappy, pursued by creditors and publishers, in order to write. An affluent Balzac might well have desisted from the literary race and enjoyed leisure, as he repeatedly wrote to Mme Hanska that he dreamed of doing. The man, his environment, and the "moment" or intellectual atmosphere around him, do help understand the novelist.

Taine laid stress on Balzac's power and acuity of observation, and justified the length of his accumulation of details. But he stressed even more two other features in Balzac: his gift for systematization and for formulating laws which organize and explain the details; and his extraordinary imagination which is the source of his "visionary genius." In the concluding sentence of his long essay, Taine ranked Balzac with Shakespeare, whose imagination he powerfully characterized six years later (in his *Littérature anglaise*) as the dramatist's "faculté maîtresse." By 1857–58, it had become current in France to praise Balzac as a "voyant." Baudelaire, whose early comments on Balzac had been rather cursory and touched chiefly on some ridicules in the behavior of Balzac the man, inserted a striking paragraph, nowadays often quoted, on Balzac as "a passionate visionary," in an article on Gautier (in *L'Artiste,* March 13, 1859). The essay was later reprinted in the Michel Lévy edition of Baudelaire's *Oeuvres* in 1868, then in *L'Art romantique* in 1925 and many a subsequent edition.[6]

IV Balzac the Realist and the Naturalist

The statistics of the printing and of the sales of Balzac's novels between 1860 and 1900, carefully established by Mr. Bellos, point to very modest sales. Not only Alexandre Dumas, Paul Féval,

Eugène Sue, but even Zulma Carraud, and George Sand with her stories of country life, far outsold Balzac. An elite of young students, Taine foremost among them, had slowly succeeded, from 1848 on, in spreading their enthusiasm for both Stendhal and Balzac. One of those who proved readiest to be fired by Taine's critical theories was Zola. He had, while evolving his doctrine on the experimental novel, read less Balzac than Taine. Still, he felt the desire to write a volume on him and to recruit him posthumously for his Naturalist school. In the early outline of his novels as he planned them in 1869, Zola announced that he was going to do for the Second Empire what Balzac had achieved for the July monarchy. That literary paternity was, naturally, intended to impress his publisher. The same year, however, 1869, Zola drafted some notes on the "differences between Balzac and me," in which he underlined his intent to avoid philosophizing as Balzac had done. His own saga-fiction would be more scientific and less social and didactic. Later, he openly regretted that Balzac had not been fully worthy of being called a "Naturalist."

Meanwhile, both Flaubert and Maupassant, although recognizing the immense power of Balzac, his range, his prophetic imagination, took exception to his style. He had not worshipped and sought beauty above all else, nor had he been able to exclude social and moral predication from his work. He had not cared enough for techniques and for style. The resemblances, if any, between *Novembre* or *L'Education sentimentale* and *Louis Lambert* or *Les Illusions perdues,* remain superficial. Maupassant's fiction owes even less to Balzac, not even to Balzac's interest in insanity and in paranoia. While Naturalism, with Zola, the early Huysmans, and others, seemed to rule over French fiction around 1880, the prestige of Balzac declined. He was only gradually, and almost grudgingly, being treated with respect as a classic. In 1876, his *Correspondance* was published, which showed harried, tortured, kindly, and naïve Balzac in a favorable light. The talk about his immorality and his lurid view of life began to subside.

In 1879, the first volume by the Belgian Viscount of Lovenjoul, who was to achieve much for Balzac's reputation and who made the accurate study of his works possible, appeared; and Cerfberr and Christophe, in 1886, offered to the Balzacians the first dictionary of the fictional characters in *La Comédie.* The first critical studies of Balzac written by academic critics — Faguet in 1887, Brunetière in 1881 and 1899 — were hesitant and vague. The celebrated statue of Balzac by Rodin, inspired by Taine's view of Balzac as embodying force, visionary imagination, commissioned in 1893, shocked the Société des Gens de Lettres when it was made public in 1898. A much more tame, classical monument to Balzac by the sculptor Falguière was inaugurated in 1902. By 1899, a hundred years after Balzac's birth, he was barely accepted in the syllabi of courses in French secondary schools; two or three of his more "classical" novels — such as *Eugénie Grandet* or *Le Père Goriot* — were admitted as texts to be dissected by candidates to the highest university examinations. Doctorate theses were not yet written, and apparently they were discouraged, on novelists of the century then dying.

V   *Slow Growth of Balzac's Reputation*

Things did not change markedly with the advent of a new century. Indeed, during the first three decades of the twentieth century, the preference of French professors, impressed by Brunetière, Faguet, Lanson, went to the classical age of French literature and only slowly moved, again with Lanson, to the philosophical works which preceded and prepared the revolution. It was a cliché of those academics to deplore Balzac's allegedly hasty and sloppy style, the length of his descriptions and picture of the nobility. Those objections did not altogether disappear from the many university theses written on Balzac during 1930–1940. But they were challenged more frequently and more forcefully. The vindication of Balzac's manner of writing has not been completely achieved as yet. But more and more critics and readers have stated their admiration for the rich vocabulary, the precision of language, the vividness and, in spite of the repeated corrections to which the novelist's proofs were submitted, for the spontaneous quality of Balzac's style. The availability of his *Correspondance* in several bulky volumes increased the admiration for his natural gifts as a writer and for the wealth of his language. By many, he was preferred to Zola and even to Flaubert.

The aspects of Balzac's work which have been studied with the greatest care are varied. For many who wrote elaborate studies of his portrayal of society, of his analysis of economic realities, his awareness of class conflicts, he appears as the supreme realist. The names of the most significant among those scholars (Barbéris, Donnard, Le Yaouanc, *et al.*) are mentioned in our bibliography.

Whatever their own political affiliations may have been, they stand in the line of Karl Marx, Friedrich Engels, and Lukacs. Whatever Balzac's own views may have been, Lukacs, echoing previous French critics, remarked that "the only men of whom the novelist writes with undisguised admiration are his bitterest political antagonists" and not the decaying aristocracy.[7] Other critics — such as Bertault, Citron, Guyon, Laubriet — have chosen to study in great detail the visionary imagination of the so-called realist, following the lead of Taine, Gautier, Baudelaire, and Béguin. They have analyzed the shifting complexities of the religious, the political attitudes of the novelist, his vision of Paris, his relations with the arts. Thorough monographs on the technique of Balzac as a novelist have been written by Madeleine Fargeaud, Suzanne Bérard, and, among the first both in date and in penetration, Maurice Bardèche. Surprisingly few have been the critics who tried to be derogatory — such as André Wurmser, Maxime Memo in *Europe,* 1965. Indeed the near-unanimity and the warmth of the special numbers of journals which celebrated the centenary of Balzac's death in 1950 (*Europe, Revue des Science humaines, Revue d'Histoire littéraire, Revue de Littérature Comparée, L'Age nouveau, et al.*) should have been disquieting. Such a glorification, coming from the most varied quarters, should have normally been followed by dissent from the younger critics. Such, however, was not the case. Since 1960, the yearly *Année balzacienne* has drawn a large number of biographers and commentators to a reconsideration of Balzac's works. Many young scholars, following upon the traces of Marcel Bouteron, Jean Pommier, Georges Castex, have produced learned and impeccable editions of many of Balzac's novels. *La Comédie Humaine* has appeared in several "Clubs du livre," inexpensive editions, and also in pocket books.

VI   *Balzac's Fame and Influence in Britain*

The reappraisal of Balzac was not limited to France and Belgium. A number of English studies appeared, among which those of Herbert J. Hunt are conspicuous for their information, their discrimination, and their wisdom. It would be preposterous to claim a strong impact of Balzac upon English novelists of this century, even when they appear to be linked to him by certain affinities — as in the case of Graham Greene, Somerset Maugham. But some of the strongest eulogies of Balzac's towering greatness as a novelist had, in the half century after his death, come from British pens. George Moore, in 1888, in his *Confessions of a young Man,* related how he first wandered through Paris, as a would-be painter, looking for Balzacian places and scenes. He never wavered in his adoration: "Upon that rock I built my church," he asserted. Balzac's range is limitless, the grandeur and the sublimity of his thoughts are beyond compare, he repeated. Almost sacrilegiously, Moore felt bold to add, "I fail utterly to see in what Shakespeare is greater than Balzac.... The work of the novelist seems to me richer than that of the dramatist."[8] Oscar Wilde, it is said, was fond of uttering his paradox that the whole nineteenth century had been the creation of Balzac. In his *Essays,* he often alluded to the suicide of Lucien de Rubempré, and praised Balzac's observation, second only to "his genius which transformed facts into truths and truths into *the* truth." He adds, more surprisingly, and in French, "Il crée un monde et se tait," creates a world and stays silent. Seldom has Balzac been praised for his silences.[9]

An American who became a British citizen, Henry James, had lauded, somewhat less controversially, Balzac's technique of "saturation." In several articles and lectures, between 1875 and 1905, he described his sense of awe in the presence of Balzac's creativeness. He saw in him both "a very bad and a very great writer," praised his vitality and his intensity. To be sure, he cannot be called a gentleman, he added; but his power is incomparable and "no more solid intellectual work was ever accomplished by man."[10]

VII   *American Scholarship and Balzac*

America did not lag behind. Several of the earliest and most thorough works on Balzac were done at Chicago, by Preston Dargan and his disciples or successors: Ethel Preston, Bernard Weinberg. A little known volume by Samuel Rogers counts among the keenest studies on Balzac in any language. A score of other scholars — among them Charles Affron, Leo Bersani, Gretchen Besser, Peter Brooks, Christopher Prendergast — have treated with originality several aspects of Balzac. Significant volumes by European creative writers have been translated and praised in America: Hugo von Hoffmansthal, Stefan Zweig.[11] It would be an exaggeration to claim that Balzac influenced the American novel of the twentieth century. Zola's fiction, at a time when Naturalism and vigorous social protest were needed to instill vitality into the fiction of Upton Sinclair, Frank Norris, John Dos Passos, Farrell, and others, was the primary foreign model, and Balzac's impact was felt through Zola's debt to him. Still, William Faulkner's creative imagination, when he lent life to the "provincial" Mississippi county where several of his tragic tales take place, was probably stimulated by Balzac.[12] Earlier still, Theodore Dreiser, in looking back at his own beginnings as a writer, related what "literary revolution" the reading of *The wild Ass's Skin* and of other Balzacian works had effected upon him. "Here was one who had a tremendous and sensitive grasp of life, philosophic, tolerant, patient, amused. . . . I knew his characters as well as he did, so magical was his skill." For several months, the young man, still in search of a direction for his literary ambitions, "ate, slept, dreamed, lived Balzac and his characters and his views and his city."[13]

Only a narrow and mechanical conception of influence in literature could lead one to detect a strong impact of Balzacian fiction upon the twentieth-century novel in France. Other forces have been at work: Tolstoy on Roger Martin du Gard, Dostoevsky on Gide; the advocates of the 1950–70 "new novel" contended that a Balzacian novel would appear an anachronism today. Influence, however, is a far subtler and more insidious process than imitation. The ambition of Jules Romains and of others in undertaking the fresco of a whole, multifarious society and of a long era is Balzacian, even if the realization of such a project falls short of Balzac's accomplishment. François Mauriac did not have to borrow any technical device from Balzac, not even his occasional obsession with reappearing characters, at times under different names, or his lurid view of provincial life. He acknowledged Pascal, Racine, Baudelaire as the builders of his soul, rather than Balzac. Still, in his preface to Claude Mauriac's volume on Balzac, he proclaimed his admiration for the range, the boldness, and the lasting verity of the Balzacian creation. His world is imbued with spirituality, even in its portrayal of abysses of vice and sin, he contended, and that is more than Mauriac was willing to say for Proust.[14] Still that Balzacian humanity is "anti-Christian in its very essence," Nietzschean in its incessant struggle for power and domination. The novels of Julian Green come probably closer to reminding their readers of Balzacian creations — *Adrienne Mesurat, Léviathan*. But the richest field for a fruitful exploration of Balzacian affinities and obsessions would be a study in depth of Proust in his relation to Balzac. Charlus, Morel, the Guermantes, the Verdurins and a score of Proustian ladies of the Faubourg Saint Germain have struck many readers as reminiscent of Balzacian characters.

VIII   *The Question of Balzac's Style*

The last among the variegated aspects of Balzac to have finally won almost unchallenged recognition is his style. It is also by far the least explored of all the provinces of Balzac scholarship. The patient inquiries into his vocabulary — the richest of any French novelist — into his syntax, his metaphors, the rhythm of his sentences, have hardly as yet been undertaken. There is not one Balzacian style, but a score of different ones: descriptive, narrative, humorous, comic and caricatural, bombastic, scientific and philosophical, starkly realistic and unabashedly mystical, poetical, and evocative. The time is past when some of Balzac's contemporaries, later followed by narrow-minded academics — such as Faguet and even Lanson — were fond of repeating that he was a bad stylist. They seemed to regret that he did not write the restrained and intellectual prose of Paul-Louis Courier or of Mérimée. Academics, like Brichot in Proust's novel, used to set classical restraint and fastidious taste above other merits of style. They for a time fell into raptures at Flaubertian cadences.

Not only M. de Charlus but Proust himself thought otherwise. The very same imaginative force and the colorful luxuriance which had been ridiculed in *Le Lys dans la Vallée* and in "La Fille aux Yeux d'Or" were bestowed the most rapturous praise by twentieth-century Balzacians. Balzac's virtue is that of saturation, which does not preclude excision, retrenchment, a tasteful selective process. His style stands at the opposite pole from the artistry of the Goncourt brothers and from the delicate vibrations and modulations of Gide's early prose. It has intensity, pliability, verve. It runs risks constantly, naturalizes strange words, invents metaphors inexhaustibly. It can be poetical and dreamy, realistic and brutal. It coins epigrams and maxims just as skillfully as La Bruyère or Benjamin Constant. Almost always, it burns with intellectual passion. Balzac spoke much less than Flaubert about the polishing of his prose and the euphony which he expected from reciting to himself over and over again his cadences. In fact he was just as

careful a worker and at least as good a master of all the resources of
the French language.

Taine, who is often represented as a dogmatic critic, remains the
only admirer of Balzac who, in his great essay on the novelist,
argued for diversity of taste in matters of style. There is, he main-
tained, an infinite number of forceful styles. The best is not neces-
sarily the one which bows to social and academic conventions.
Balzac's versatility as a master of prose may at first bewilder us like
a "fantastic chaos," he says. Soon the mind and the heart are won
over by the swarming of ideas, the profusion of metaphors. He
concludes, "Oriental poetry has nothing more dazzling or more
luxuriant; it is a luxury and an intoxication; . . . all the voluptuous
delights of summer days enter the senses and the heart. . . . That
man, whatever may have been said to the contrary, knows his
language; he knew it as well as any one else, but he put it to use in
his own way."[15] The more attentively Balzac's mastery of prose is
studied by specialists, the more confirmation of Taine's judgment
is likely to be provided.

Notes and References

Chapter One

1. *Letters to Mme Hanska,* Vol. I (Delta), p. 527. All letters to Eva Hanska refer to this same edition. The translations are mine.
2. Honoré de Balzac, *Correspondance.* Editor, Roger Pierrot. (Garnier, 1960), Vol. I, p. 60.
3. *Ibid.,* Vol. II, p. 182, letter from Zulma Carraud dated 28 November 1832.
4. *Opus Cit.,* Letter to Mme Hanska, February 15, 1934, Vol. I, p. 38.

Chapter Two

1. *Ibid.,* letter to Laure Surville dated August 1832, p. 89.
2. Along with Ernst Curtius's admirable volume teeming with insight on Balzac's thought, the most detailed and comprehensive work on Balzac as a thinker is that of the Danish scholar Per Nykrog (1965). The most specialized study of *Louis Lambert* and Balzac's philosophy is that of the English critic Henri Evans. See bibliography.
3. T S. Eliot, "Shakespeare and the stoicism of Seneca," (1927), in *Selected Essays* (New York: Harcourt Brace, 1932).

Chapter Three

1. Letter written on September 30, 1832, *Correspondance,* II, p. 141.
2. *Ibid.,* February 20, 1830, p. 253.
3. *Ibid.,* August 27 and September 2, 1833, Vol. II, p. 344 and p. 355.
4. Albert Camus, "L'Intelligence et l'Echafaud," in *Problèmes du Roman.* Jean Prévost, Editor. (Lyon, 1943), p. 220.
5. *Correspondance,* Vol. I, pp. 269–70.
6. *Ferragus,* Pléiade Vol. V, p. 26.
7. The two scholars mentioned published their discovery in a detailed and fascinating article, "La véritable Eugénie Grandet," in *Revue des Sciences humaines,* New Series, No. 80. October-December 1955, pp. 437–58.
8. We shall observe here in passing that ladies connected with Balzac seem to have been all endowed with long life. Both his mother and his wife outlived him, and Zulma Carraud was over ninety when she died in 1889.
9. *Correspondance,* Vol. II, p. 390.

Chapter Four

1. The book dates from 1834. In 1839 Balzac corrected his text, published by Béchet, and prepared a new edition for Charpentier with many minor changes. In 1841 he signed a contract for Furne for the whole *Comédie Humaine* in 12 volumes. *La Recherche* will be Tome XIV of that edition — again with minor changes, mostly stylistic. For a full discussion and thorough study of the work, see Madeleine Fargeaud's *Balzac et La Recherche de l'Absolu*. (Hachette, 1968).

Chapter Five

1. See, among others, Maurice Bardèche's *Balzac Romancier,* in which all preceding works are presented as a genesis and preparation for *Père Goriot.* Also, Herbert Hunt's *Balzac's Comédie Humaine,* p. 86.
2. See Pierre Barbéris's *Le Père Goriot de Balzac,* p. 25.
3. The comparison with Shakespeare's *King Lear* was made early in the *Courrier Français* (April 15, 1835). For further possible sources, see Castex's introduction to the 1963 Garnier edition of *Père Goriot.*
4. *Letters to Mme Hanska,* Vol. I, p. 257, Letter dated 18 October 1834.
5. *Balzac: Le Père Goriot,* p. 14.

Chapter Six

1. *Correspondance,* Vol. II, p. 655, letter dated 10 March 1835.
2. Those influences or affinities have been exhaustively traced by Moise ie Yaouanc in his erudite introduction to *Le Lys* (Garnier, 1966), and by Jacques Borel in his monograph, *Le Lys dans la Vallée* (Corti, 1961).
3. There is an original study by Victor Brombert on the play of names in the novel — Blanche, Henriette (the two names of Madame de Mortsauf), and Natalie: *Mouvements Premiers* (Paris: Librarie Joseph Corti, 1972), pp. 177–90.

Chapter Seven

1. See in this connection Fredric Jameson's interesting article, "The ideology of form: partial systems in *La Vieille Fille,*" Madison: *Substance,* No. 15, Winter 1976, pp. 29–47.

Chapter Eight

1. The author of the most learned scholarly book on *Les Illusions perdues* is Suzanne Jean-Bérard: La Genèse d'un Roman de Balzac: Les Illu-

sions perdues, 2 vols. (A. Colin, 1961). She treats only the first of the three volumes of the novel. She goes so far — unwisely, it seems — as to suspect "a latent Sodomy" in Balzac's affection for the young men whom he often protected and liked to mold.

2. That powerful, lurid tragedy, reminiscent of the violent Jacobean drama, had much impressed Balzac. Its theme came from a historical work by the French Abbé de Saint-Réal (1674). The play, much admired by Byron, was repeatedly acted in England and France until the middle of the last century. The courtesan Aquilina was one of the characters. Jaffeir was spelt Jaffier by Balzac.

3. In *Le Monde de Balzac* (Arthaud, 1973), and previously in *Balzac et le Mal du Siècle* (Gallimard, 1970, 2 vols.), and in *Mythes balzaciens* (A. Colin, 1971).

Chapter Nine

1. Jean Hytier. "Un Chef d'Oeuvre improvisé: La Cousine Bette," *The Romanic Review,* New York: April 1949, No.", p. 92.

Chapter Ten

1. One, by Arlette Michel, was not available to me when this book was concluded: *Le mariage et l'Amour dans l'Oeuvre romanesque de Balzac* (Paris: Champion, 1976).

2. For a genesis of the novel see the recent Pléiade edition of 1976, Vol. I, pp. 169–80.

3. See in this connection M. Fargeaud's article, "Laurence la mal aimée," in the 1961 *Année Balzacienne* and, in the 1964 volume, "Un beaufrère de Balzac," by Havard de Montagne.

4. Pierre Abraham has written an interesting book on this subject. See in our bibliography *Créatures chez Balzac.*

5. *Lettres à Mme Hanska,* II, p. 156, letter dated 22 January 1843: "I would rather be a Russian than any other subject. The Czar, being sole sovereign and master ... fulfills all my ideas on politics which, in its essence, is expressed by the words: a strong power in the hand of one only." The statement on Louis XVI occurs in the same volume II, p. 440, in the letter dated June 2, 1844.

Chapter Eleven

1. One of the champions is Albert Arrault, in *Madame Hanska. Le dernier amour de Balzac.* (Tours: Arrault, 1949).

2. H. Hunt, *Balzac. A Biography.* (London: Athlone Press, 1957), p. 168.

Chapter Twelve

1. Vol. I, p. 269, letter dated October 26, 1834.

2. Letter to Hippolyte Castille, in *La Semaine,* October 11, 1846. Reprinted in Balzac's *Oeuvres Complètes,* Ed. Guy le Prat of the Societé des Etudes Balzaciennes, Vol. 28, 1963, p. 495.

3. Preface to *Le Cabinet des Antiques,* 1939, Pléiade XI, p. 368.

4. "Lettre sur la Littérature," July 15, 1840, in *Revue Parisienne.* Reprinted in *Oeuvres Complètes,* Vol. 28, p. 86.

5. Georg Lukàcs, *Studies in European Realism.* (New York: Grosset and Dunlap, 1964), p. 42.

6. "Traité de la Vie élégante," *Oeuvres Diverses,* Vol. II, p. 161.

7. Jean Hervé Donnard, *Balzac. Les Réalités économiques et sociales dans La Comédie Humaine.* (A. Colin, 1961), p. 442.

8. Louis Chevalier, *Labouring Classes and dangerous Classes in Paris during the first half of the 19th Century.* (London: Routledge and Regan Paul, 1973). The French original appeared at Plon's in 1958.

9. F. Engels, *Sur la Littérature et l'Art.* (Paris: Editions Sociales, 1954), p. 320.

10. The allusion to *The Curé de Village* refers to statements such as "If the industrial product is not worth twice its cost in cash, commerce would not exist." Pléiade VIII, p. 716.

11. Harry Levin, *The Gates of Horn.* (New York: Oxford University Press, 1963), p. 213.

12. Michel Butor, *Répertoire I,* "Balzac et la Réalité." (Paris: Edition de Minuit, 1960), p. 89.

13. Balzac asserted that he himself was the possessor of the secrets contained in his characters — and, therefore, the interpreter of his own "hieroglyphics." See Pléiade XI, p. 174.

14. The most comprehensive and helpful study in this respect is that of Geneviève Delattre, *Les Opinions littéraires de Balzac.* (Paris: P.U.F., 1961). The most detailed on Balzac's affinities with his great predecessors from Touraine is by Maurice Lécuyer: *Balzac et Rabelais.* (Paris: Belles Lettres, 1956).

15. See Chapter XIV of his *Craft of Fiction.*

Chapter Thirteen

1. David Bellos, *Balzac Criticism in France, 1850–1900.* (Oxford: Clarendon Press, 1976).

2. Article in *Le Peuple,* August 21, 1850, quoted in David Bellos's book, p. 29.

3. Quoted in Bellos's book, p. 119. The subject of Balzac's high standing with Marxist thinkers is broad and little explored. Among Marx's many allusions to Balzac in his voluminous work, there is a letter dated February 25, 1867, written to Engels, in which a few remarks on the play

Mercadet are followed by the advice to read "Le chef d'oeuvre inconnu" and "Melmoth réconcilié." "Those are two short masterpieces full of a delightful irony." *Correspondance Marx-Engels.* Editeur: Alfred Costes, 1934, Vol. IX, pp. 136–37. Friedrich Engels praised Balzac to a British novelist and socialist, Margaret Harkness. In 1883, while sick, he enjoyed reading nothing but Balzac. To Laura Lafargue he wrote, "The pleasure which that big chap ('ce grand bonhomme') gave me was complete. There is French history from 1815 to 1848 . . . and what boldness, what revolutionary dialectics in its poetic justice." Lukacs's essays on Realism, written in a Marxist context, give close attention to Balzac: *Studies in European Realism.* (New York: The Universal Library, 1964).

4. Article published in *La Tribune* on October 31, 1869.

5. The article appeared first in several sections of the *Journal des Débats* of February and March 1858, and was reprinted soon after in Brussels, along with several articles by Théophile Gautier on Balzac, then in Taine's *Nouveaux Essais de Critique et d'Histoire,* Hachette, 1864, pp. 63–170. It was translated into English by Lorenzo O'Rourke in 1973, (New York: Haskell House).

6. The subject of Baudelaire's view of Balzac, of the awe in which he stood of Balzac's willpower and imaginative force, of his oft expressed desire to turn into a novelist, of his admiration for Balzac as a Swedenborgian, then as an epic painter of modern life, has not been adequately treated. As early as 1846, in concluding his *Salon* of that year, Baudelaire exalted Vautrin, Rastignac, and Birotteau above the heroes of the *Iliad.*

7. G. Lukacs, *Studies in European Realism,* p. 44.

8. George Moore, *Confessions of a young Man.* (New York: Brentano, Second Edition, 1898), pp. 72–73.

9. Oscar Wilde, *Essays,* Vol. IV of his *Complete Writings.* (New York: The Nottingham Society), pp. 77–81. Wilde spent the end of his life in a modest lodging in Paris where he had registered as "Monsieur Melmoth."

10. The chief text by James in this connection is "The lesson of Balzac," first delivered as a lecture, then published in August 1905 in *The Atlantic Monthly,* and later reprinted in his book, *The Question of our Speech.* (Boston: Houghton Mifflin, 1905).

11. Zweig, in several studies on Balzac, places him among "die Baumeister der Welt" — the builders of the world. Stefan Zweig, *Balzac.* Translated by W. and D. Rose. (New York: The Viking Press, 1946).

12. William Faulkner declared, to students who questioned him, "I read some of Balzac almost every year." *Faulkner in the University,* Eds. Fred Gwynn and Joseph Blotner. (Charlottesville: University of Virginia Press, 1959), p. 50. In order to explain why Sherwood Anderson had, in his opinion, missed greatness, Faulkner said that "he didn't have the ruthlessness to rob from any source, . . . he probably didn't have a concept of the cosmos in miniature which Balzac and Dickens had." pp. 231–32.

13. Theodore Dreiser, *A Book about Myself.* (New York: Boni and Liveright, 1922), p. 411.

14. Claude Mauriac, *Aimer Balzac.* (Paris: Table Ronde, 1945).

15. The third section of Taine's essay on Balzac is devoted to the novelist's style. Among the few attempts at a systematic study of Balzac's use of adjectives and of metaphors, the pioneering work of Gilbert Mayer remains suggestive: *La Qualification affective dans les Romans de Balzac.* (Geneva: Droz, 1940). It was succeeded by a highly technical study by Lucienne Frappier-Mazur, *L'Expression métaphorique dans La Comédie Humaine.* (Paris: Klincksieck, 1976), and, by the same author, "Aspects baroques du paysage métaphorique dans *La Comédie Humaine.*" (*Cahiers de l'Association internationale des Etudes françaises,* No. 29, May 1977, pp. 81–98). In an earlier volume of the same *Cahiers* (No. 15, March 1963), there had appeared an essay by Francis Bar on "Balzac styliste," pp. 309–30. The most useful suggestions for a bold study of Balzac's style were offered by Henri Mitterand in "A propos du style de Balzac," *Europe,* 43rd year, Nos. 429–30, January-February 1965, pp. 145–60. For an example of the passionate partiality with which French critics like to judge their great writers, praising one against another, see Claude-Edmonde Magny, *Lettre sur le Pouvoir d'Ecrire,* (Paris: Seghers, 1947). Flaubert's claims to being a good writer are exploded by the vehement critic, who derides him as "a brother, hardly less stupid, of Bouvard and Pécuchet," while Balzac's epic resonance and mastery of style are raised to the skies.

Selected Bibliography

PRIMARY SOURCES

There have been, especially since the upsurge of Balzac studies that followed the first centenary of the novelist's death in 1850, a large number of editions of *La Comédie Humaine,* many of them expensive and not easily available. A number of novels were then published by the Garnier publishing house; these are critical editions, prefaced by expert scholars, providing variants and informing footnotes.

The one convenient and widely available edition, found in most libraries, is the eleven volume Pléiade edition, to which our references are given: the volume and page number appear in parentheses; all translations are ours. The eleventh volume contains, besides the *Contes Drolatiques* not discussed in our study, the important prefaces by Balzac or inspired by him, and two invaluable indices of real persons and of fictitious characters in *La Comédie Humaine.* For the sundry essays such as "Des Artistes," "Code des Gens honnêtes," "Lettre à Charles Nodier sur la Palingénésie humaine," our references are to volumes 38 and 39 (1835 and 1838) of Balzac's *Oeuvres Diverses* published by Conard.

Our quotations from the correspondence are from the following editions, both done with admirable care by Roger Pierrot: *Correspondance,* Garnier, five volumes: Vol. I (1809-32), 1960; Vol. II (1832-35), 1962; Vol. III (1836-39), 1964; Vol. IV (1840-45), 1966; Vol. V (1845-50), 1969. *Lettres à Mme Hanska,* Paris: Editions du Delta, 3 Vols.: Vol. I (1832-40), 1967; Vol. II (1841-June 1845), 1968; Vol. III (Aug. 1845-March 1847), 1969.

Nothing would be gained from listing Balzac's novels and stories within the general groupings assigned to them by the author: "Scènes de la Vie parisienne," "Scènes de la Vie de Province," "Etudes Philosophiques," etc. Balzac altered his classification repeatedly, assigned the novels to one or another category, often for reasons of salesmanship. The dates mentioned here are equally untrustworthy, since Balzac first published many of his works in daily or monthly papers, then as books, then rewrote parts of them, freshened up some of his stories to bring them more up to date or because his own ideas had been altered.

The early novels which Balzac had himself refused to include in *La*

175

Comédie Humaine, some of which have received disproportionate attention from recent scholars, are not included in the following list:

1829. *Physiologie du Mariage,* began as early as 1824, then altered.

1834. *Les Chouans.* Originally appeared as *Le dernier Chouan,* 1829. Between 1830 and 1832, several short stories, or "Etudes," incorporated into *Scènes de la Vie privée* and *Etudes Philosophiques:* "Le Bal de Sceaux," "La Vendetta," "El Verdugo," "Une Passion dans le Désert," "Le Réquisitionnaire," "L'Auberge rouge," "Une double Famille," "Un Episode sous la Terreur," "La Maison du Chat qui pelote," "La Bourse," "La Paix du Ménage," "Une double Famille," "Gobseck," "Le Message," "Adieu," "L'Elixir de longue Vie," "Le Chef-d'Oeuvre inconnu," "Les Proscrits," "Jésus Christ en Flandre," "La grande Bretèche," "Maître Cornélius," "Le message," "Sarrasine," "Madame Firmiani," "La Grenadière," "La Femme adandonnée."

1831. *La Peau de Chagrin.*

1832. *Le Colonel Chabert.*

1832-33. *Les Marana.*

1833. *Le Médecin de Campagne. Ferragus. L'Illustre Gaudissart. Eugénie Grandet.*

1832-35. *Louis Lambert.*

1834. *La Recherche de l'Absolu.*

1834-35. *Le Père Goriot. La Fille aux Yeux d'Or. La Duchesse de Langeais* (first called "Ne touchez pas la Hache"). *Séraphita.*

1835. *Le Lys dans la Vallée.* "Melmoth réconcilié." *Le Contrat de Mariage* (first called *La Fleur des Pois*).

1835-36. "Les Martyrs ignorés." "L'Enfant maudit." "Un Drame au Bord de la Mer." "La Messe de l'Athée." *La Vieille Fille.* "Facino Cane." *L'Interdiction.*

1837. *Les Employés. César Birotteau. Les Illusions perdues* (I). *Gambara.*

1838. *La Maison Nucingen.*

1839. *Massimilia Doni. Les Illusions perdues* (II). *Une Fille d'Eve. Le Cabinet des Antiques* (1836-39). "Les Secrets de la Princesse de Cadignan." *Béatrix* (I). *Le Curé de Village.*

1840. "Z. Marcas." "Pierre Grassou." "Un Prince de la Bohème." *Pierrette.*

1841. "La Fausse Maîtresse." *Ursule Mirouet. Une ténebreause Affaire. Catherine de Médicis, begun in 1831, in three parts.*

1842-43. *La Rabouilleuse. Mémoires de deux jeunes Mariées,* written for the most part in 1825-33. *Un Début dans la Vie.* "Autre Etude de Femme." *Albert Savarus. La Muse du Département. Honorine.*

1844-45. *Modeste Mignon* (written earlier). *La Femme de Trente Ans* (begun in 1831). *Béatrix* (II). "Gaudissart II." *Les Paysans* (left unfinished. Completed by Balzac's widow, published in 1855).

1846. *Les Comédiens sans le savoir, La Cousine Bette.*

1847. *Le Cousin Pons. Splendeurs et Misères des Courtisanes* (written between 1839 and 1847).

1848. *L'Envers de l'Histoire contemporaine* (begun in 1842).

1854–55. *Les Petits Bourgeois* (begun in 1845, second half done by Charles Rabou). *Le Député d'Arcis* (begun in 1847, continued, very poorly, by Charles Rabou).

SECONDARY SOURCES

The following list of critical works on Balzac could easily be expanded to include essential articles and very specialized works. It has been purposely limited to titles which are fairly recent and, because they are either in English or in French, are easily available in libraries. All the French volumes here mentioned, unless stated otherwise, were published in Paris; only the publishing firm, therefore, is mentioned.

ABRAHAM, PIERRE. *Créatures chez Balzac*. Gallimard, 1931. On the physical description of Balzac's characters and the relationship between the "physique" (eyes, hair, nose, neck) and the spiritual characteristics. The sources and the working of genius according to Balzac, his fascination with Gall and Lavater.

AFFRON, CHARLES. *Patterns of Failure in La Comédie Humaine*. New Haven: Yale University Press, 1966. How and why failure becomes an implacable necessity in Balzacian fiction. Laws affirmed by Balzac: growth and decay, greatness and decadence. The destructive power of the intellect. The irony of degradation in passionate characters.

AMBLARD, MARIE CLAUDE. *L'Oeuvre fantastique de Balzac. Sources et Philosophie*. Didier, 1972. Treats an original and seldom discussed aspect of Balzac's imaginative fiction.

L'Année Balzacienne. From 1960 on: one volume a year. Indispensable for the wealth and precision of its articles on Balzac's life, acquaintances, sources, variants, unfinished sketches.

ARRIGON, L. J. *Les Années romatiques de Balzac*. Perrin, 1927. Distant and cool relations of Balzac with the Romantics between 1820 and 1830. Anecdotic and lively, only moderately reliable.

BALDENSPERGER, FERNAND. *Orientations étrangères chez Balzac*. Champion, 1927. A survey of Balzacian plots, episodes, characters, touching on non-French countries. Learned, enlightening on many details. The role of foreign works which influenced Balzac: Arabian Nights, Sterne, Scott, Cooper.

BARBÉRIS, PIERRE. *Balzac et le Mal du Siècle*. Contribution à une Physiologie du Monde Moderne. Gallimard, 1970. 2 vols. A colossal undertaking, with a Balzacian subtitle and an immense energy, reaching only to the year 1833 in 1,988 pages. Three more volumes are promised. The author does not hide his passionate partiality. The "mal du siècle" is viewed as a form of man's Promethean revolt against fate.

_____. *Mythes balzaciens*. A. Colin, 1972. Series of considerations on Balzac as a royalist; democracy and freedom, the idea of order in Balzac, the new bourgeoisie.

_____. *Balzac. Une Mythologie réaliste*. Larousse, 1971. (Collection, Thèmes et Textes). Larousse, 1971. A lively survey of several aspects of Balzac's work, especially its realism and the fortune of Balzac's novels with critics and the public in the twentieth century.

BARDÈCHE, MAURICE. *Balzac Romancier. La Formation de l'Art du Roman chez Balzac: 1820–35*. Plon, 1940. An essential and detailed study of how Balzac learned his craft, from his earliest attempts, through the genesis, structure, and originality of *Le Père Goriot*. Sober and penetrating analyses.

_____. *Une Lecture de Balzac*. Les Sept Couleurs, 1964. A general view of the several aspects of Balzacian fiction, for the nonspecialist: comprehensive, done with taste and warmth, with many original remarks on individual novels.

BARRIÉRE, PAUL. *Balzac et la Tradition littéraire classique*. Hachette, 1928. Balzac in his relationship with Classical comedy (Molière), Classical tragedy; especially on the novelist's obsession with Tartuffe which he wanted to redo in a modern setting.

BEEBE, MAURICE. *Ivory Towers and sacred Founts. The Artist as Hero in Fiction from Goethe to Joyce*. New York: New York University Press, 1964. Part II. "The novelist as creator" places Balzac as the portrayer of artists, Mabuse, D'Arthez, Bridau, among other novelists, one of them being Henry James, author of *The Sacred Fount*. Much less thorough than Laubriet on the same theme.

BÉGUIN, ALBERT. *Balzac Visionnaire*. Geneva: Skira, 1946. A remarkably perspicacious, accurate presentation of the several aspects of Balzac's personality and work. Reappeared in 1965 at Le Seuil, Paris, under the less felicitous title of *Balzac lu et relu*.

BELLOS, DAVID. *Balzac Criticism in France. 1850–1900. The Making of a Reputation*. Oxford; Clarendon Press, 1976. A detailed survey of the slow growth of Balzac's fame.

BERSANI, LEO. *Balzac to Beckett. Center and Circumference in French Fiction*. New York: Oxford University Press, 1970. The first of five chapters discusses Balzac, praises some novels and dismisses others. The angle of approach is that of the novelist's loss of confidence in the expressiveness of language. Highly theoretical and haughtily abstract.

BERTAULT, PHILIPPE. *Balzac et la Religion*. Boivin, 1939. A very thorough and relatively objective treatment of Balzac's attitudes toward religion, by a Catholic priest.

_____. *Balzac, l'Homme et l'Oeuvre*. Boivin Hatier, 1946. A concise and good general presentation of the diverse facets of the man and his main works.

BESSER, GRETCHEN. *Balzac's Concept of Genius*. Geneva: Droz, 1969. The enigma of genius as permeating Balzac's fiction; the novelist's thirst for omniscience and omnipotence. The essence of creativity according to Balzac, and the role of woman as the companion of a man of genius.

BILLODEAU, FRANÇOIS. *Balzac et le Jeu des Mots*. Montréal: Presses de l'Université, 1971. Balzac's novel (especially *La Peau de Chagrin*) is studied as an architectural complex of words and sentences in which the form coincides with the meaning.

BONARD, OLIVER. *La Peinture dans la Création balzacienne*. Geneva: Droz, 1969. Balzac's obsession with visual effects, from his early stories onward. How his style fuses the pictorial manner and the caricatural effects.

BROOKS, PETER. *The melodramatic Imagination*. New Haven: Yale University Press, 1976. The Balzacian novel in its relation to popular literature: strong emotionalism, extreme situations, good and bad opposed to one another, taste for excess and forceful passion are the features common to the melodrama and to some of Balzac's novels.

BUTOR, MICHEL. "Balzac et la Réalité." *Nouvelle Revue Française,* August 1959, 228-47. Reprinted in *Répertoire,* I, Editions de Minuit, 1960, 79-93. One of the keenest, and most admiring, essays on Balzac by a novelist of the 1960s. Balzac's solution to the problem of how to convey reality in the novel is seen as offering new paths to the fiction of 1960-70.

CANFIELD, A. G. *The reappearing Characters in Balzac's Comédie Humaine*. Chapel Hill: North Carolina University Press, 1961. A methodical and perceptive study of the famous device, less thorough than Pugh's subsequent work.

CASTEX, PIERRE. *Le Conte fantastique en France de Nodier à Maupassant*. Corti, 1951. The standard work on the fantastic tale. The chapter on Balzac (pp. 160–213) is the first important work on Balzac by one who became the most active and eminent Balzacian in France.

CITRON, PIERRE. *La Poésie de Paris dans la Littérature française de Rousseau à Baudelaire*. Les Editions de Minuit, 1961. Chapter XXII in vol. 2 (pp. 181-237) is devoted to Balzac as a portrayer, analyst, and painter of Paris.

CURTIUS, ERNST ROBERT. *Balzac*. Translated from the German by Henri Jourdan. Grasset, 1933. (German original, Bonn, 1923). To this day, one of the most profound studies of Balzac, envisaged through a series of chapters on mystery, energy, passion, politics, religion, romanticism, etc.

DELATTRE, GENEVIÉVE. *Les Opinions littéraires de Balzac*. Presses Universitaires, 1961. An exhaustive and valuable study of Balzac's opinions, as expressed by himself directly or through his characters, on French and non-French writers, Rabelais, Molière, Cervantes, Otway, Rousseau, Scott, Stendhal.

LAUBRIET, PIERRE. *L'Intelligence de l'Art chez Balzac.* Didier, 1961. The most thorough and the most sensitive of the many studies on Balzac and art.

————. *Un Catéchisme esthétique. Le Chef d'Oeuvre inconnu de Balzac.* Didier, 1961. An exhaustive study, textual and philosophical, of the celebrated short story.

LÉCUYER, MAURICE. *Balzac et Rabelais.* Belles Lettres, 1956. A rich treatment of the analogies between the two authors and of Balzac's immense debt to his predecessor.

LEVIN, HARRY. *The Gates of Horn: a Study of five French Realists.* London: Oxford University Press, 1963. (Chapter IV on Balzac, pp. 150–213). A perceptive and suggestive elucidation of the quality of Balzac's "realism."

LE YAOUANC, MOISE. *Nosographie de l'Humanité balzacienne.* Maloine, 1959. The most thorough exploration into medical science at the time of Balzac, and into the role of diseases (physical, mental, nervous) in his fiction.

LOCK, PETER W. *Balzac. Le Père Goriot.* London: Edward Arnold, 1967. One of the best brief monographs on a novel of Balzac, with precise and acute remarks on the style.

LORANT, ANDRÉ. *Les Parents pauvres.* Geneva: Droz, 1967, 2 vols. On the genesis, sources, prototypes of the characters in *La Cousine Bette.*

LOVENJOUL, SPOELBERCH de. *Histoire des Oeuvres d'Honoré de Balzac.* Calmann Lévy, 1875. The great pioneering work which served as a basis for all subsequent scholarship on Balzac.

LUKACS, GEORG. *Balzac et le Réalisme français.* Traduit de l'allemand par Paul Laveau. Maspero, 1967.

————. *Studies in European Realism.* Introduction by A. Kazin. New York: Grosset and Dunlap, 1964. Chapters 1, 2, and 3, on *The Peasants, Lost Illusions,* and Balzac and Stendhal. A very warm apology for Balzac's realism, placed much higher by the Hungarian critic than Flaubert's, Zola's, or any other "realist" in the novel.

MCCORMICK, DIANA FESTA. *Les Nouvelles de Balzac.* Nizet, 1973. The only systematic work on Balzac as a short story writer.

MARCEAU, FÉLICIEN. *Balzac et son Monde.* Gallimard, 1955. A survey of the varieties of characters created by Balzac, by a twentieth-century novelist.

MAUROIS, ANDRÉ. *Prométhée ou la Vie de Balzac.* Hachette, 1975. Translated by Norman Denny as *Prometheus: The Life of Balzac.* New York: Harper and Row, 1969. A substantial, lively biography, fully up to date in its documentation, quoting generously from Balzac's correspondence.

MÉNARD, MAURICE. "Fécondités balzaciennes: 1970-76." *Stanford French Review,* 1, 2, Fall 1977, pp. 261-74. An excellent critical survey of works (mostly French) on Balzac from 1970 on.

MICHEL, ARLETTE. *Le Mariage et l'Amour dans l'Oeuvre romanesque de Balzac.* Champion, 1976. An extensive treatment of an immense and momentous theme, a study that is profound and sensitively done.

MILATCHITCH, DOUCHAN Z. *Le Théâtre de H. de Balzac.* Hachette, 1930. The one comprehensive study of the least successful of Balzac's literary attempts (one omitted in our volume).

NYKROG, PER. *La Pensée de Balzac dans La Comédie Humaine.* Copenhagen, Munksgaard, 1965. The most systematic attempt to do a synthetic presentation of Balzac's thought.

PICON, GAËTAN. *Balzac par lui-même.* Seuil, 1956.

PRENDERGAST, CHRISTOPHER. *Balzac. Fiction and Melodrama.* London: Edwin Arnold, 1978. A very skillful and convincing rehabilitation of Balzac's melodramatic fiction.

PUGH, ANTHONY. *Balzac's recurring Characters.* Toronto: University of Toronto Press, 1974. An extremely scholarly volume, inevitably dry and overabundantly factual, on the evolution of the device of reappearing characters after 1834-35. It shows how Balzac gradually saw and utilized richer possibilities in that device. Over 500 pages.

ROGERS, SAMUEL. *Balzac and the Novel.* New York: Octagon Books, 1969. A very good and incisive study of Balzac as a novelist.

TAINE, HYPPOLITE. *Balzac. A critical Study.* Translated by Lorenzo O'Rourke. New York: Haskell House, 1973. A recent translation of the best critical essay written on Balzac in the last century. It appeared in *Nouveaux Essais de Critique et d'Histoire* in 1865.

WURMSER, ANDRÉ. *La Comédie inhumaine.* Gallimard, 1964. (2nd ed., 1970). One of the few volumes on Balzac consistently out of sympathy with him. Done with brilliance, in 806 pages.

ZWEIG, STEFAN. *Balzac.* New York: The Viking Press, 1946. A smooth, sensitive, and fair biography, parts of which had appeared in German under other titles (e.g. *Baumeister der Welt*) and in French as *Balzac, Le Roman de sa Vie.* Albin Michel, 1950.

Index

Place names and names of fictional characters are not included. In listing alphabetically, definite and indefinite articles, and the prepositions *à* and *de* have been ignored. *La Revue de Paris,* for example, is listed under *R (Revue)*.

DATE DUE